Record

Issue 9, 2021

Record Mascot Merch

now available at
record-magazine.com

Editor-in-Chief
Karl Henkell

Senior Editor
Michael Kalenderian

Art Director
Holly Canham

Design
Javi Bayo

Editorial Assistant
Campbell Bews

Logo Design
Andrew Woodhead

Cover Image
Matilda Hill-Jenkins

Contributing Photographers
Patricia Casten, Emma Le Doyen, Lyndon French,
Ruby Harris, Matilda Hill-Jenkins, Kyle Knodell, Ian Lanterman,
Nils Müller, Ulysses Ortega, Tanya and Zhenya Posternak

Illustrations
Elijah Anderson, Jean Jullien, Nadine Redlich

Contributing Writers
Terry Craven, Glen Goetze, Kiloran Hiscock, Brandon Hocura, Bruce Tantum

Special Thanks
Hannah Canham, Kayhl Cooper, Marc Teissier du Cros, Marc Davis,
Honey Dijon, Mark Farina, Brian Foote, Sam Holt, Alexis Le-Tan,
Public Possession, Alicia Prior, Colin Self, Tim Sweeney

Publisher
Record Creative Limited
First Floor, Penrose 1, Penrose Dock, Cork, T23 KW81, Ireland
+353 21 234 8513   Company No. 660437

Printing
KOPA, EU
ISSN 2711-9920
–

Contact us for distribution, advertising, special projects,
or just to say hello at info@record-magazine.com

Record Culture Magazine
New York / Berlin / Madrid / Melbourne

DAHSAR

COMMERCIAL

Subscribe!

Just like with records, you can almost never have enough.
record-magazine.com/subscribe

While dance floors have been empty, the deeply
interconnected ecosystem that is the music world
has shown itself to be remarkably resilient and adaptable
in the face of a global pandemic. A community spirit
— which has always been present — has grown in volume
to meet the moment, with a wave of campaigns to support
artists, shops, venues and their staff through tough times,
hoping to sustain them so that they're all still around
as the world's stages slowly begin to reopen.

"Going live" and endless video calls haven't replaced
real connection. And as the fatigue from isolation and
lockdowns grows stronger, so too does our anticipation
for a return to the dance floor after our longest break
in memory. We're already planning our party outfits.

Karl Henkell
Editor-in-Chief

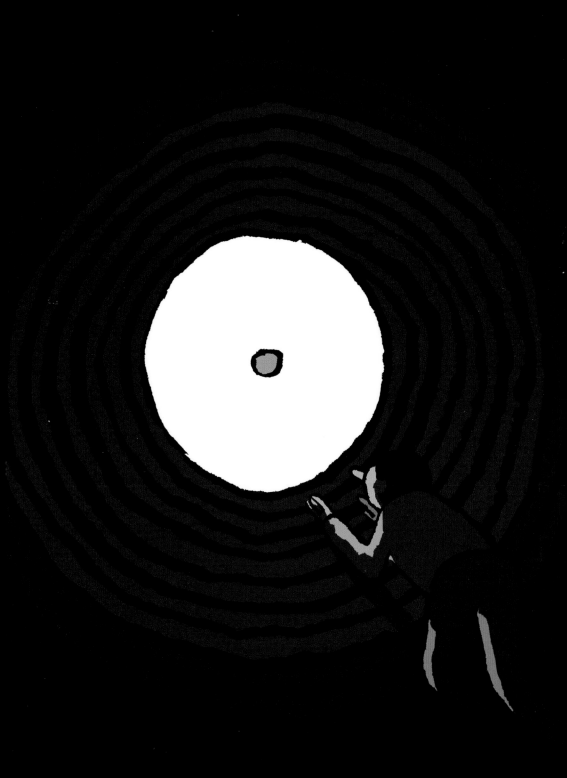

Bradley Zero

You might know Bradley Zero as the DJ with the infectious smile, the former host of Boiler Room, or quite likely from Rhythm Section, the record label that's been gaining seemingly-constant momentum from its home base in Peckham. Once upon a time, Zero aspired to be a visual artist, but music proved to be his lasting passion. Now that Rhythm Section's influence in the dance music community is growing, as well as his own, Zero is using his label and NTS radio show to shine a light on others.

Interview – Terry Craven
Photography – Matilda Hill-Jenkins

Record

You grew up in West Yorkshire playing drums, and starting to play gigs. How did that influence your first notions of what it is to put a show on?

I mean, my first memory of doing any kind of event was when I just started to learn how to play drums, and there was a battle of bands at school in Wakefield. All I remember doing was a Metallica cover, "For Whom the Bell Tolls." [*laughs*] And that was very much just sticking our feet in the water. There's two things that led to the first gigs I put on. The first one was realizing that I enjoy dancing. Sounds weird, but I always thought of it as this annoying thing that you kind of — I remember that transition from, like, being a kid and not understanding it, to, I don't know, coming into myself a bit. You know, my memory of dancing before I was like 14 or 15 was just being dragged onto the dance floor by your mum at a wedding. You know, like pretending to go through the motions and just being like, "What is this?" Or even before that being a kid running around a village hall, like, in circles, as fast as you can.

And there was something that clicked that was separate from just like trying to, you know, dance with girls or snog someone at the year 9 ball. Moving just became a joy, rather than something that you just go through the motions of. That was a major step, that, I don't know why or how it happened, but there's just something that clicked, where I realized that I liked and enjoyed dancing, just for the sake of dancing. Not as like some mating ritual, but really as just like an expressive exercise. So I think that was the first early breakthrough into this journey of putting on and creating dance music.

The second one was, I was a drummer, so I was putting on gigs in sixth form. And I don't often think about it because we didn't approach it like a business in any way. I think we got paid like 30 quid to split between us, even though we were actually bringing in hundreds of people. There were two bands in our school, basically, who were like the bands, and it was an event when we played and it felt like most people in the year came out. They were small venues, but it was packed, you know?

But it was really just an opportunity at that time to do the thing that you've been doing in each others' bedrooms and garages in real life. Huddersfield had quite an interesting, and very supportive — well, supportive in the sense that there was lots of opportunities to play, not supportive in the sense that someone was making loads of money off all these kids. [*laughs*]

> "There's just something that clicked, where I realized that I liked and enjoyed dancing, just for the sake of dancing."

Your dad was a DJ and owned a record store in Bradford. Are there any memories that stand out for you? Obviously seeing your father doing this sort of thing day in and day out must kind of seep in?

Yeah but "seeps" is the word, because it's not this groundbreaking moment where you see something that changes your life or your direction or your desires, it was just something in the background constantly. It wasn't like I was just a kid whose dad was a doctor, and then one day I went to a club and it was like, "Whoa." I was growing up around records, around speakers, around XLR cables, around my dad's lighting, playing with microphones, setting up CDJs and turntables in like the '90s, you know what I mean? It was just something that was there. And when it's just there, and when it's just your dad doing his work in his office or in his storage unit, it wasn't something that was like, "Whoa." It was mundane. So I never had a desire to, or even the thought to follow in those footsteps and do this thing that I found really exciting. It was just something that was there that just seeped into me, you know?

And do you think seeing your dad grafting, day-in day-out, gave you a balanced perspective of DJ'ing and the music business?

I think a lot of people from the outside see this job of DJ'ing as like super glamorous, and, really, just like glitzy, and they only see when you're on stage, or the Instagram photos of you coming off a private jet, not that I'm ever on a private jet. But you know what I mean, that's the layman's vision of a DJ. For most of my life until I was maybe 14, 15, my dad's office was in our house. He was working, he was going out to the post twice a day, he was writing emails, going through paperwork, chasing invoices. I guess I would have subconsciously linked this idea of diligence and office work to DJ'ing, which I guess is something that most people, if they didn't grow up around the realities of that, have a different idea.

There is a lot of romance in it, and I don't want to suck that out of it. Because there's some real magic that can happen. There are some very pinch-yourself moments, but I think the thing that allows those moments to keep happening, and builds a solid foundation so that things can grow and develop and opportunities arise, is the really mundane stuff, the really boring stuff; the contracts, paying people on time, really thinking about quantities and really pushing a record in terms of promotion, because, what's the point? There's this attitude in a lot of very small labels where it's like, "underground," and they'll want to do 300 limited edition records with no repress, no digital, maybe not even a name on the label. And I think that's kind of cool in the sense of collecting something that is so mysterious and rare and just a one-off. But you've got to ask yourself, "What's the purpose in that?" Are you trying to share something? Are you trying to spread the word? Are you trying to give the art the best chance it can to get out there? Or is it just a little vanity project that's just for you and a few friends? It becomes a rich person's game, because you're in quite a privileged position to be able to just do something with the ultimate goal of just breaking even. You can't do that if you actually want to pay people, you can't do that if you actually want to make it something that you can do for a living or support other artists. So my aim from the start was really to treat it like, I have a mission, you know. That's the way I approached it.

You've said your first ever records collected in Yorkshire were actually lost, having melted on the window ledge. So was it after moving to London that you really started collecting records?

I'd started before; I started wanting to be a scratch DJ and I'd bought a bunch of battle records and beats and samples and just unknowingly left them in front of the window and the sun refracted and melted them all, so that was the end of my illustrious scratch DJ dreams. My DJ QBert phase. I was probably about 14 or 15 then. I got a little collection before I went to London and then it's when I moved to London, I really started putting some serious time and energy and money into it. And it's just like, how can I describe it? It's a strange pastime, isn't it? To collect an antiquated medium, and spend all your money on something that you don't really need.

I get the feeling it has a lot to do with like, building a home for ourselves, in an intellectual sense. Creating your domain.

Yeah, but it's your domain so much to the point where someone else could come into that domain and see an absolute mess. And you see a castle, you see the turrets of records and the wonderful sunlit uplands of vinyl. And to me, it looks beautiful, whether they're stacked on the floor, or whether they're falling out of a shelf, or lined up against a corner of the wall. I don't see mess, that's what's strange. I think there's

> "Are you trying to give the art the best chance it can to get out there? Or is it just a little vanity project that's just for you and a few friends?"

"At one point, you couldn't step on the floor, because it was just full of records."

an element of, like, delusional behavior when it comes to collecting, because you tell yourself you need it, you tell yourself that it's good for you, that you're one step closer to achieving that thing that you'll never really achieve. It's a funny old thing. And having lived with housemates, I saw those visions clash a few times, because I'd lived in my house before I moved to where I am now, where I have my own record room, I was sharing a lounge with four people. And at one point, you couldn't step on the floor, because it was just full of records. I'd really have to have people to tell me that it was becoming a nuisance. Kind of, like, you know, you see these old men, and it tends to be old men, in, you know, "Britain's Worst Hoarders" on ITV3.

There's a little bit of that, but the difference is I think hoarding is a very solitary activity. Whereas the idea of collecting things, coming together to play them and to share them and to compare them and to actually make something happen in real life with them. I think that's the key thing. It goes back to the community thing and that is the thing that keeps you going. And, you know, a lot of the records that I pull out here, there's a memory associated to it, which was in some dance floor in some place where something special happened, and you

don't get that with digital files. You don't hang out and compare WAVs, they're too ephemeral, you know? Why bother doing that when you could just download it? But an item that you maybe found and that you can't get anywhere else or that isn't readily available or has a bit of history to it. That's something that brings people together and that's what it's about for me.

I was reading about Rhythm Section being vinyl-only most of the time, and how you'd said it forces DJs to go through their entire collection of records. Why is it important to go through your entire collection?

Just reminding yourself of what you've got, and transporting you back to that place. And when I'm playing a Rhythm Section party — so I do play digitally, certainly for radio, and when I'm traveling in places I don't know — but when it's my own parties, we stick to the rule of just vinyl. In preparation, I literally go through everything, and there's no organization. I really don't know what I'm looking for or what I'm going to get. So it becomes this kind of pick and mix, lucky dip scenario, where it will always be like a total surprise. And a thread will emerge as I start to go for the things that pull me in at that moment.

> "More often than not, when you're forced into a corner and you have to take a risk, that's when the magic happens, you know."

And you trust yourself to know that's going to happen?

Well, I trust the collection, in that I know that there's enough stuff here to weave a narrative, to make something happen. But when it comes down to the actual night, and to the actual performance, the difference when you're playing with a set amount of records is that technically, it's a lot harder. So you really have to be a lot more engaged and focused and at one at that moment, because you don't have the BPMs, you don't have the key, you can't see visually how long the intro is or how long the outro is, or whether there's a break in the middle, you know — if you're loading something up on a CDJ, you can see all this just like in a kind of waveform — so you have to be switched on. But then what it does, is it forces you to really think, and you might want to get from A to C, and you've got 100 ways to do it, but maybe only one of them works. And more often than not, when you're forced into a corner and you have to take a risk, that's when the magic happens, you know. And not to say the magic can't happen with digital, it absolutely can. But you're just less inclined to take that risk because it is a risk. And why would you take a risk when you don't need to? If you know it's something that will work, you probably just go for the thing that will work. But if you

have no other option than to try this thing and, "Oh, I'm not sure if it's going to fit or if it's gonna clash," that's when something will happen that's totally unexpected and not only surprise the people there, but surprise you, and that's what keeps that fun.

Do you consciously choose the radio as a place to hold space for other artists to showcase stuff that you've been sent constantly?

I think when I started out on radio, I was playing more records and it was more a reflection of my archive as much as it was my contemporary discoveries, like new music. But yeah, on the radio, especially, it's definitely gone more towards a platform for sharing new music, giving artists that are coming up a break, giving the first plays of new music that I've received from friends and peers. That's what it's become, and it's kind of helped sharpen my focus of what my mission is, you know. I remember when I first heard my first release played on the radio, you know, when Gilles Peterson played Al Dobson Jr. It was just this moment of like, "Wow." Hearing it on the airwaves presented in the context of someone like that, almost giving it the thumbs up was just such a big moment and such a big boost.

"The only way you're going
to do the best you can do is
by being true to what's around
you when you're starting out."

It's easy to overlook the importance of the platform that I've got because I might think of it as just a tune I've played on the radio, but for someone else that might be the first time they've had someone legitimize what they've been doing. There's a lot of responsibility there. But it's also just like, such a huge honor to be able to do that. And that's what my radio show is, basically.

You've previously said that starting a record label isn't an ethical choice, but I think in your case it actually might be. You're working with people to build a community, while paying attention to what's ahead.

Absolutely. And I think when you start that is an important thing, because it is important to see what's around you, and no one else can tell your story better than you. So why try and mimic what someone else did? It's great to have inspirations, it's great to have role models, and it's great to have a label or a publisher that you look up to, but if you're going to do it your own way, you have to do it your own way. And the only way you're going to do the best you can do is by being true to what's around you when you're starting out.

But something I've grown to understand as the project has grown and expanded beyond this very local, narrow focus is that as a platform — and this is true in I think a lot of different situations, whether it's a business or a publishing house, or a radio station or anything — as it grows, you do have a bit more responsibility to look outside your immediate circle. And this is a trap that I'm ever more aware of falling into as we grow, because it can easily just be like, you and your mates doing your thing. And then as things grow you can find yourself in a position where you've just created this homogenous collective. Or this like, very undiverse catalogue. Because, you know, when you're starting out, and you're literally just engaging [with] what you see around you, that's fine, isn't it? Because you don't have a duty to represent a wider community if you're just one person doing one record or two or three, but by the time you've got 20 or 30, or 40, or 50, and you have a kind of international following, then I think you do have to start to look outside of your bubble. And this is something that I've become more and more aware of with Rhythm Section, and something that we are trying to remedy. Because I think what people might often forget is that there's no master plan when you set out to do something like this. You're just like running with the blinkers on, just doing what comes easy and what comes natural and what's there. I think we've got to a point now where we need to be more aware of the bigger context of the music industry and be a lot more diverse and look down avenues that perhaps we haven't had to in the past. Because we've been surrounded by a certain kind of thing. And now we need to expand on that.

"I think we've got to a point now where we need to be more aware of the bigger context of the music industry and be a lot more diverse and look down avenues that perhaps we haven't had to in the past."

DEATH F

Record

you know, and there's also a huge imbalance of men running the show behind the scenes. It's a difficult thing to talk about, because it is what it is, and it's not going to change overnight. And as much as you become aware of that, and kind of want to start to address that, it's a slow process, you know. So this is one part of the conversation that we want to start with the "SHOUTS" compilations. I mean, it was called "SHOUTS" for a number of reasons, but it's to shout about stuff that we're into, to give a voice to people that haven't had the chance, or to forge connections with people that we want to work with in the future, but just by doing, like, a one-track-at-a-time kind of thing. And the other side of what we wanted to do to address this is through the mentorship and the Patreon scheme, and the studio program.

At the same time I don't think of Rhythm Section as some radical political agenda or a label who puts the politics and these causes front and center. Because it's not what it started out as, it's not what I want it to be, you know. But at the same time, I don't just want to imagine everything's OK, and that there's not something we can do to, you know, to change the conversation and to level out that playing field. I think some people are more inclined to be outwardly political, and, you know, to engage in these debates on social media. Whether it's on Twitter, on Facebook, whether it's, you know, just not quite in the real world, but in the virtual world, in the social arena. Some people do that very well, some people made that their focus. There's a lot of great labels who have emerged in the last year or so, they're pushing for these things, through their music and through their releases. And it's front and center of what they do. But I also think it's kind of a shame, certainly as a Black person, as a minority, being forced to make your project about that, you know?

And that's not to take anything away from anyone who decides to make their project or their output directly relating to these issues. But I think it's a shame when that's almost all you can do, and so much creativity is funneled into just one specific lane. The way I want to approach this is like, rather than trying to make something change overnight is to address the root causes, you know. We have an imbalance of male producers on our roster. It's not going to change overnight, but what we can do is make extra effort, and allocate extra time, and put resources and funding and, you know, mentorship hours into getting more women in the studio. And prioritizing those who have been left out of the picture for far too long. But it's not something that I feel like shouting about because it just becomes this cacophony of virtue signaling, everyone kind of somehow proving that they're holier than someone else. So I'd rather be doing my bit in the background to try and make a difference, and also, I just think being a visible person in this role is a step forward. **R**

> "At the same time I don't think of Rhythm Section as some radical political agenda or a label who puts the politics and these causes front and center."

What are the next steps for you?

So we did this "SHOUTS" compilation last year, and it was a chance to work with a lot of artists at once, and to present a lot of new artists, a lot of new connections, in a way that we haven't had the chance to do before. Because what we've done up until that point was just, you know, EP, album, EP, album, EP, album, just big projects. Never a V/A, which means various artists, never singles. The music was generally coming from the community that existed around us, arguably the status quo. Which, you know, in the last few years has been thrust into the spotlight as something that was extremely unbalanced in terms of gender and race, you know? So almost unknowingly, we've been just reflecting the status quo, because that was what was there. And that was what we were a part of, even though I'm, you know, there's not many — just to put it bluntly, there's not many Black people running labels in this kind of realm. There's a few really good labels, like, Black-owned, but [it's a] huge minority,

Sébastien Tellier

Sébastien Tellier is a shape-shifter, a chameleon continually adapting to the times. Growing up outside Paris, Tellier's meaningful encounter with contemporaries Phoenix and Air kickstarted his music career, and over the years he's carved out a niche among his contemporaries, with a nod to French soundtrack composers of the past. With each album, Tellier inhabits new worlds and tongue-in-cheek characters, giving himself the starring role in the stories of his own creation.

Interview – Karl Henkell
Photography – Emma Le Doyen

Did you grow up in Paris?

I had a kind of special youth, because I grew up not inside Paris, but in the suburbs of Paris. Maybe 30 kilometers from Paris. It was the first fresh, brand new city in France. Just before it was fields. And they decide to create a fresh new city, like in the U.S., like flat with a center, with modern buildings, and all around big suburbs with all the same houses and little gardens and blah, blah, blah. So I grew up in this city. But the city was not finished, it was always in construction, and just [beyond] the city, it was the real countryside, the field. So it was a very strange ambience. It was really good for a kid because I did a lot of BMX and skated a lot. And it was so flat. And so new. It was great, you know, for skate. So easy to ride. It was special. And at the same time, I knew Paris is not so far. And sometimes, with my parents, I went to Paris. And it was so old with strange lights everywhere. And so I grew up in this kind of ambience, like, close to Paris, but not in Paris. In a very weird city.

It sounds like someone trying to build a modern utopia back then.

Yes, yes. But it was without political ideas. It was just a new city, to try to be new, to be fresh, to be attractive. To create an attractive *pôle* [center], something like that, you know. It was more commercial than a political, or philosophical utopia. It was a business.

Could you be in the countryside very quickly?

Yeah. Countryside was, riding my bike, it was maybe five minutes, you know? And it was quite cool because I remember a lot of rides in the forest. And a strange sport zone, like a huge rugby ground. But it was empty because all the apartments, the houses was not full. It was not bought yet. So it was super strange.

Was there music around you when you were growing up? What were your parents listening to?

It's clearly my dad, [who brought] me on the way of the music. My dad is really passionate with the guitar. He's a rhythmic guitar player. Like, super serious. Even if it's not his business or job he's more professional than the professional. And the passion of my father was the complexity of the chords. And so, very often, he took his guitar, he gave me a guitar, and we played together. And he did show me all the complicated chords, and all the, you know, very sensitive variation of chords and blah, blah, blah. And so my dad bring me in this adventure. And at home, we listen to a lot of Pink Floyd. It was the favorite band of my father. He described Pink Floyd as gods. So I grew up with the idea [that] Pink Floyd is not just a regular person, or musician. But David Gilmour for me was a god. And so David Gilmour had a huge influence in my youth. And when I was a teenager, I tried to be the same, with long hair. So at home, every Sunday, in the morning, we listen to Pink Floyd. Like mass, in a

religious way. It was deep. And beside Pink Floyd, we listened to a lot of the French radio, which is the pop music from France. And, my father did buy a lot of 45s. All the little singles, so, [*sings*] "Video killed the radio star." A lot, a lot, a lot. And, you know Billy Joel...

Did you learn piano at a young age, or any other instruments?

I start [with] the guitar at 6. I had an imitation of a Fender Stratocaster. It was a small black Nashville, but for kids, and it was great because it was possible to plug it, you know into an amplifier, with the distortion, you know. More fun than the piano class. So it was great, but I did it, like, with my father during the weekend sometimes, and after I had my first real electric guitar, but with adult size, and so with this guitar, it was a Hohner, an imitation of a Telecaster. I love this guitar, and so, with this guitar, I really start to play guitar with a passion. It was around 9. But in the same time, besides that, I had a drum [kit] in my bedroom. It was great, the same age, 9, 10. And after I have a few synths, but cheap, not vintage synths like Yamaha, not the DX7. And so at around 12 I had a home studio in my bedroom. But it was very rare. It was kind of unique because back in the day it was not so easy to have a home studio.

And so at around 12, I start to do demos, few synths, guitar, and try to record the drum. But it was really difficult to record the drum with one mic. And so that was the beginning, because my father at Christmas, it was not so much toys, but the gift was, more guitar, drum or synth, so step by step I had quite a lot of music stuff. For my dad, it was an obsession [that] I become a professional musician. It was really an obsession, he wanted it strong. And so I did that, because I really loved that. When I remember my first demo at home with the 4-track recorder on little tape, it's very, very good memories, it was great. It was kind of magic, like guitar, after you put the melody after you put a few chords of the synth, I was involved, I was excited.

In that doco ["Sébastien Tellier: Many Lives"] about you that came out recently, your friend talked about how you lived in an apartment without a window at around 20. Can you describe that reality? What was your life like at 20, before all this started?

It was crazy because I come from — so my mum's a teacher, my father was working in the cosmetic industry, but not very high level, and so I was in a kind of, if we talk about the ambience of your life, I was in a kind of average state. But when I came from the weird suburb to Paris I was quite lucky because I had this room, but without a window. And I was very poor. And in Paris, it's really hard to be without money because everything is expensive. I remember there is a shop close to my room, it was a *traiteur*, so it's a food shop with beautiful half avocado with shrimp and

"At home, we listen to a lot of Pink Floyd. It was the favorite band of my father. He described Pink Floyd as gods."

mayonnaise inside the hole. And I was dreaming about that, but it was too expensive. And I never bought it, but every day I saw this fantastic avocado. And I remember that because my life was like that. Paris was full of beautiful shops, luxurious shoe shops, luxurious girls, cars around, but it was impossible to do. I was super frustrated, for me it was painful. And my apartment was dirty, full of garbage, and totally — my life was like a dog, you know? Just on the sofa, ham and chips, a lot. And I played a lot of guitar because [I had] nothing else to do than play guitar. So I was always in front of my TV, but with no sound from the TV and I played guitar watching the TV almost all the day. And with a few friends around like, "Oh, I like this chord."

And it was a strange life and very savage with a lot of LSD, MDMA, cocaine. Dirty and drugs, it was terrible, but in a way, I didn't have the choice because if you want to do music in France, you have to be in Paris, you can't be, I don't know, far from Paris, because all the business is in Paris. So I had to be in Paris, but it was the first step. When you don't have money, and you don't have a girlfriend or any glam side of your life, to take drugs is like you just stay in your apartment, but it's a great night, it's, "Wow, it was crazy," but you just stay in your apartment. Super pitiful, but it was my life. I'm not proud about my choices at this period. I mean it was tough. And I was really sad, so it's a time I prefer to leave behind.

"And, for me, it was not a choice. I was just sure to do it. Even if I have to play in the streets. But I was sure I will be a musician."

You moved to Paris with the idea of doing music. So being there was your first step?

Yes, it was important for me to be close to show business. Even if it's just French show business. But it's important to feel the same thing, to understand the rules, the codes, to try to go to a party with people working in the industry, blah, blah, blah. But, at the end, I never see no one, because I did my demos during this, in this little room with no window. And after, I went to a record company to propose my music. And at the very first rendezvous, the guy said, "OK, we will give you a deal, we sign you." So I went to Paris to meet people and blah, blah, blah. And actually, I didn't do it. And I didn't have the time to do it because, at my first rendezvous, it was OK, it was done.

Back then did it feel like you had no other option than to become a musician? Is that how it felt, that you had to make it in music or else what were you gonna do?

Yeah, but for me, it was important to live in music. I hate the regular rules like, "Oh, you have to be at 8 at the office." At this time for me, it was impossible to be just a regular person at the office with a suit. And for me, to be a musician was a freedom, an idea of freedom. I was thinking that because I was without knowledge. Because to be a musician, it's a lot of work. You have to travel, you have to be at the studio, you have to fix the mix. It's hard to be a musician, but at this time, in my head, it was like, "For sure it's musician because it's freedom. I can wake up at noon, I can drug myself, I can drink a lot of alcohol, all the beautiful girls, spend my days [thinking] about culture, and blah, blah, blah, the culture of the music." And it was with this kind of life, I was sure to make music. So it was, first my dad wanted [that] I become a musician. Then I was super involved. And, for me, it was not a choice. I was just sure to do it. Even if I have to play in the streets. But I was sure I will be a musician.

Did you already know guys like Air and Phoenix back then, or were they people you looked up to?

No, because at my very first rendezvous with the record company, Phoenix was in the corridor. And so I met Phoenix like that, at the very first rendezvous, "Hello." "Hello." With very good clothes, like super good style, super cool guys, like, "Wow." I went to this rendezvous with my best friend, Mathieu Tonetti. He did two videos for me. And after — very fast because I had a deal on the first day — the guy of the record company, organizes a meeting between me, Phoenix, Air, Daft Punk. Not organized but bring me to the party and so maybe in one month, I knew all the guys. Cassius, Daft Punk, Air, Phoenix and Rob [Coudert]. It was very fast. It's a few weeks, so I have very, very good memories of these times because I was happy. It was really, in my mind, the beginning of my life. Like, OK, I have cool friends, not drug addicted, cool guys, winners...

That are doing stuff.

Smart and cool, and so for me, it was great. It was really great to meet these guys. I learned so much from Phoenix, from Daft Punk, from Air because I was a kind of dirty, crazy savage, and they allow me to be polite. And, you know, how you have to move in a party or to say hello, and blah, blah, blah.

Because after I was in the party, like already [had a] whiskey bottle before the party. Breaking everything in the kitchen. So with them, I calm down, I said to myself, "Ah, OK, these guys, they are so cool and they are calm." It's a calm ambience, polite. And so I said to myself, "Ah OK. I want to be like that." And so, they [taught] me, what is a good synth. Air, they [taught] me a lot about synthesizers, "Choose this one, not this one." How to do the bass with the synths, the Minimoog, all the good synths, because I had synths but not the really good ones. So it was great, because it was a new life with super cool people, and one day Phoenix did their first big tour in France, like I don't know, maybe 40 gigs. And I came to the front of the tour bus to say, "Oh, have a good tour." And just before the bus leaves Paris for the tour, they say, "Come in the bus, come with us." And I go in the bus, and then I did all the tour with them. But doing nothing, you know, just as a friend and a spectator. But it was this kind of time, very often together and a lot of fun, blah, blah, blah. So it was great. It was one of the best parts of my life.

"My first professional gig was, I think in Dallas, in a first opening band for Air. But in front of 30,000 people."

And pretty quickly, didn't you launch straight into a tour with Air in the U.S.?

It was very, very fast. It was crazy because I never did professional gigs in my life. And so I did two gigs in Paris, very, very weird with 30 people, in a very little cafe, Le Duc des Lombards. And so my first professional gig was, I think in Dallas, in a first opening band for Air. But in front of 30,000 people. And it was cool because it was [exciting], it was in the U.S. But that was really stressful because I was scared. Before the show, I was very, very [stressed], le trac [stage fright] in French. But at the same time, it was great because with this tour, it was not just the U.S., it was Europe, Japan. I discovered the world through Air. Because [they] bring me everywhere around the world, but I discover the world in a very good [style], like success — I was not the successful band, but with Air, through [their] success, the beautiful hotels, beautiful tour bus, beautiful everything, and beautiful invitation at the party, and great ambience. Air was really on the top of their career, you know, it was like crazy, millions of record sales, blah, blah.

I went to LA once and New York once, but before that, I did not really know the U.S. It was cool to discover all the cities of the U.S. between New York and LA. And the same for Europe, Stockholm, Denmark, Madrid, Portugal, and it was great, so, yes, this time, I felt very lucky, like, "Whoa. I'm so lucky to be there. I'm so lucky to discover this world." And it gives me a lot of knowledge about the world, and a lot of knowledge about what is the life of a real musician and what is a tour. How to do an interview. So it was great. It was maybe the best part of my career.

In the years preceding your first album "L'Incroyable Vérité," did you have lots of time to think about what you wanted to do?

Yes, because I spent so much time in this little room without windows. I was always playing guitar. I was always thinking about what kind of artist I want to be. And so, not hip-hop, because I don't have the skills, I don't have the shape of a hip-hop guy. No. I'm French so, no rock, because French rock, it's terrible. It's something from the Commonwealth, English people, I don't know, but not French. And so I had one cool option as a French guy. It was music for movie, soundtrack guy. So, Michel Legrand, François de Roubaix, [Georges] Delerue, these kinds of guys. OK,

as a French, it was cool to be like that. You know, kind of strange, mysterious guy doing super good soundtracks. So at this point of my life, a long time ago, in terms of style and in terms of role of an artist character, it was like a soundtrack guy, like long hair, have a beard, strange clothes, strange guy, and I choose this direction, in terms of style, not trying to be a U.S.-style or with a cap or, no, I wear a lot of cap, but like super French, like French compositeur, it was my style. And so it was matching with my compositeur because, first, I feel in my music, the best I can give is my composition, my chords, and my melody. So it was matching a lot to this kind of artistic character with my real way to create the music, so I'm not a producer. I never had MPC, it's always with the piano, guitar, and chord, blah, blah. So, I choose that this time, Daft Punk is a robot, Air bourgeois, Phoenix U.S.-style and me, it was the French guy.

Did these contemporaries help light the path for you?

It was great, because it was, you know, before this kind of band, it was almost impossible to release a record in English for a French band. All the record companies ask — at this time, long time ago, 20 years ago — the French artist to sing in French.

And so, with Daft Punk, Cassius, Air, they opened the way to, yeah, if a French guy sings in English, he can be a star or successful. I was very grateful about that because, for me, it was, "Wow. After all these years of jail, it's the freedom." For me it was great because even if I was a small artist in terms of success compared to them, we were all in the same bus. It was the same adventure, you know? Because, like I say I was in tour with Phoenix, but with nothing to do, but for me, it was maybe better than to be on scène [stage]. And OK, Air, I was opening band, it was not me, but it was the same. It was great for me because I did "L'Incroyable Vérité." It's a very, very strange record, very dark, very complicated, very intellectual. So it was not first possible for me to go on the U.S. radio, and, you know...

With that record.

But for me in my mind, I had the best of both [worlds], because I did my very personal and purely artistic music. But I had the glamour and the fun of the commercial, of — not commercial music, because they don't really do commercial music, but, you know, the success, the glamour, the good parties. So for me, I still feel exactly this sensation. I just take the best of the parts I like, and I'm OK like that. I don't have the need to be a huge star, and you know, if I have to go somewhere, I take my personal aircraft, I don't need that. Because I like to be *tranquille* [quiet], you know? And to live without pressure, with not so much responsibility. I really like that. I feel good like that. I feel I found great balance, *équilibre*.

Are you a product of your environment? Is your sound or performance influenced by Paris or France in general?

Yes in a way, because, like I say, when I choose my character as an artist, I always choose what kind of music I want to do as a French guy. So to be French had a big impact on the art of my music. For me, it's really important to create a good relationship because the reality of your person and your music, you know, because my name is Sébastien Tellier so I released my record as Sébastien Tellier and so, with this name, Sébastien Tellier, a very, very French name. It's weird to do [*mimics a rock & roll band*]. It's not matching, it's not a beautiful painting. My goal was to create something where everything is matching.

So to be French was important, but not necessarily in Paris. It could be Côte d'Azur, Cannes, it could be Biarritz, Le Pais Basque near Spain. Paris is not important for me. But to be French was really, really important for me. It was really important for me at this time to do very French music. So "L'Incroyable Vérité," my first album, is very French. And after I opened the doors because France is too small, and the world is so big full of beauty, so I opened the door. But at this time, it was important for me to be super French.

Is France big enough to be successful as a musician? Can you exist as just a French musician, or did you have to go beyond?

I think you have to go beyond. I mean there are some very successful French singers in France at the stadium, like Johnny Hallyday. But I don't know, it's more like, yeah, no, it's possible. It's possible because France, it's still a very cultural country. And there is a lot of space for art in general. I mean, there is a lot of rehearsal rooms. A lot of bars you can play. A lot of venues, theater, blah, blah, blah. So it's OK. But it's not super fun to be French and just to have a French career. It's not so fun. For me, it was really exciting after I did my own tour in the U.S. with "Sexuality." It was great. You feel bigger. [*chuckles*]

It was cool. And, because France is, OK. It's full of culture, but it's small, you know. So your tour is just two or four hours from Paris. And so maybe that could be a little ridiculous you say, "Hey, I'm going on tour," but it's just...

One hour away.

But with the U.S. and Japan, it's a long flight. "I'm on tour, yeah." So it's more stylish, I guess.

"It's a very simple technique, I wait to miss the piano."

What's the process of writing a new album or song for you? Does the concept have to come first?

Usually it's starting from the need to play piano. I see the piano, so I want to play. And I need to play, and sometimes, I play something, [that rings] a bell you know. I play everything like [*sings*], with no idea. Kind of working somewhere with no goal. I don't really check my hands, but at one point if I hear something with some interest, I watch my hands, I say, "Ah when I do that [*mimes playing*], OK." And it's just that and it's just three notes, and after, I build something from that. But it's really natural, very easy, nothing special. I did that a lot. I have a lot of little pieces of music, and beside I'm on the sofa, I think about what I would like to do, and what could be the next station of the music, you know. And so when I have a good idea of what I want I just listen to all my little parts, hundreds of little parts and I say, "Ah, this little part could be a good [base] for what I want to do."

And so it's kind of freedom in the piano, and thinking on the sofa, and after there is a kind of wedding of that, *voilà*. Usually, I don't push myself to compose. I wait to have the real need to play piano. It's always better because if you really need it, you find something. But if you push and push yourself to find something, it's a nightmare. Then it's like mud, you know? And so it's a very simple technique, I wait to miss the piano. And, after it's I guess the regular way to compose.

Is the piano your most important writing instrument?

The piano is good because you can play [for a] long, long time. You can play four hours of piano. It's OK for the fingers, but the problem with the guitar is that after one hour of guitar it's really painful. It's terrible. So sometimes to compose a song, you could take five minutes, of course. But sometimes it's much more. Sometimes I spend two weeks to compose a song. And so I can't spend eight hours on the guitar. It's impossible, it's too painful. Because of that, it's a lot with the piano. But I'm not a good piano player. I play piano like a child. Very simple part. But it's good because I play a lot of piano, but not in a technical way. I play piano just for the beauty of the chord, I maybe find the melody and blah, blah, blah.

But it's always very simple. So it's not eight hours of [*mimes frantically playing piano*], it's eight hours but quiet and soft, so the piano is good because the piano could be strong, or it could be super soft. It's very large with 88 notes, you know. And for me the piano is also a kind of eternal instrument, because it matches very well, for example, with Daft Punk, when there is piano on Daft Punk, it's modern. But also piano in Mozart, or I don't know, Beatles. It works with all kinds of music. The last hit of BTS. It's "Dynamite." It's a huge hit, and there is piano in it. And so, the piano is really magic because it matches with everything, and you can also compose reggae with the piano. It's great. The piano, it's a great door opener.

It seems that the piano always has a place in your music.

It's not my choice. Because OK I play piano at home because it's my way to compose. But it's more the guy who did the video. Like, "Wow, we have a great idea. We would shoot you playing piano." I say, "OK, but it's not..." I don't ask to play piano on the video, it's always the guy or MTV for the promotion. They always ask me, "Bring your piano," and I say "OK, if you want." But it's not my obsession.

So that doesn't come from you necessarily?

No, not at all from me. Piano in terms of image, it's not my obsession at all. In a way, I don't really like that, it's too much Elton John, the piano, I like a lot of songs of Elton John of course, but I like to be in the front and sing my song, like I don't know, George Michael, or Michael Jackson, or Madonna, you know?

People take me and put me in this piano situation. But it's not my choice. And I did a song named "La Ritournelle" and it's maybe my biggest song, I guess, and it's full of piano. And so, I think, *voilà*, it's the mind of the people they say, "But he played a lot of piano because this song is full of piano." But it's not a choice, it's just like that...

It's just people needing to put you in a box—

Yeah, yeah, yeah.

—to understand you.

The box of the piano player.

I heard that in the past, and maybe you still do this, you sell all your equipment in your studio after each album, essentially dismantling your studio. Can you explain this habit? Is it so you don't repeat yourself?

It's really important to — it's a question of being respectful of the audience. For me, it's really important to propose something totally new, for example. My last album, "Domesticated," it's totally — not the opposite, but, of my album before named "L'Aventura," it's not at all the same goals, and for me, it's important to do that because the audience is really sensitive, and they feel everything through the notes. And so they know when the guy is lazy, or when the guy just does another song because, well, he needs to do another song...

> "I change my apartment, I change my car, I change my clothes to be fresh, new, to really propose something different"

I change everything. It's new sounds of synths, it's new sounds of bass, new sounds of guitar. I don't sing at all the same way with my voice. I can't change my voice, but I really try to find another way, and I change my apartment, I change my car, I change my clothes to be fresh, new, to really propose something different, and it's really hard to change [your] whole mind. But it's quite easy. It's not really easy, but it's possible to change everything around you. It's just another jacket, another apartment, or OK another synth. It's possible. It's possible, so I do it. And for me, it's great because it's not a usual artist life, like, "OK. I go to my studio." It's always different for each album, it's totally a new adventure and it's important. And for me, it's almost a duty in front of my audience, because it's important. Sometimes, for example, you're Australian, but AC/DC, it's a huge band and fantastic band. But for me, it's always the same Gibson on the same amplifier [*sings and mimes playing AC/DC*]. I love it. It's great, it's fantastic. It's strong art and very monolithic art in a way it's fantastic, and so I don't judge or anything.

"I'm the god of my music, and I want to stay like that, because it's my own world."

But for me, it's boring to do that, with the same Gibson in the same amplifier. No, I want new synths. When I buy a new synth, it's like, "Whoa," like it's a circus in my head. It's great to have new stuff. It's great also to have a new apartment. When you change your neighborhood, it's great. New shops, new life, new ambience. It's really great. It's something really important to be happy, to change often. I guess it's also because of my personality. I'm quickly bored. I'm quickly, like, "OK, what's next?" I don't know why, but I'm like that.

So you go further than just changing your equipment, you change your apartment, your clothing, and your car, even.

Yes, it's really important. Because it's a new life. For each album it's a new life. But it's also like a big celebration of the new album. You know, it's not like, "Oh I do another album." It's a new life. It's a new universe. But it's important and again, I'm not a band, I'm just myself. And so when you're alone, it's hard to excite your mind. You know, if you talk with someone, it's, "Wow," it's super. It's electric. But if you're alone it's stuck, and so to change everything around me, I'm alone, yes but it's OK, I'm excited.

Is being alone important to you, in the writing process?

I don't know why, but I guess the world is so crazy, and I have [no] influence on the world, so my music, I can control it, I can put everything where I want, it's my little theater, perfect little box, you know.

I'm the god of my music, and I want to stay like that, because it's my own world. So that's why I love to do music alone because it's mine. It's just mine, you know, even if after I work with producers and on stage I play with guys. And it's always a pleasure to work with other people, it's great. But most of the time, I'm alone, but I really like that and when I compose, I don't like at all to compose with someone else, it's terrible. To produce with someone else, yes, it's great, but to compose, I really need to be the master of my little construction.

Does new equipment, vintage synths and so on, give you ideas through their unpredictabilities?

Ah, yes, yes. It's great because when you have new sounds, the sounds themselves create a way for a composition. I mean, the guys who built the stuff of music are so important in music. The Moog synthesizer, Oberheim, Fender, Gibson, all of these brands, guitar or synths, are all very important, even the brand who invent the MPC drum machine. They are the real genius, you know. It's not the musician because after, OK. You plug it [*mimes playing music*] and boo boo boo and you have pleasure. But it's magic to create this kind of instrument. And so it's not enough honor for these kind of guys. They are worth celebration, it's really important. So, it's really important to have new stuff, new toys, in a way. And it's like my daughter, when I give a new doll to my daughter, she invents a new adventure, because it's another doll, with another story. And it's exactly the same with the synth with another sound. It gives you the need to do another chord, or another tempo, and blah, blah, blah. So yes. For me, it's really important. Even if I play a lot of piano, if I need something else, there is always a synth, and you just [*mimes playing synth*] bum, bum, bum, bum, bum, you find something.

Do you ever hear the entire song in your head before playing it? Like was that the case of "La Ritournelle"?

"La Ritournelle," it was quick. I bought my [Yamaha] CP-80 and it was in my little room without a window. And I wake up and I went to the piano, and I play it, but when I play it, I play the song straight. I didn't search anything, the song came to me like that. It could happen very often to every kind of artist. But this one, it was very straight, very short. And so, it was really easy to compose this one. No problem. After some times, you can find a good following of chords, but after one minute, it's going, so you have to find another *truc* [thing] and sometimes it's hard, because it's always easy to find the A passage, but it's always very difficult to find the B part, you know, because if you go to the piano and you're lucky, you find something very good. But after, you have to work to really search something, as an intro, as an outro, to find a verse, or to find a chorus. And so for me I can spend five minutes to compose the songs, but three weeks to compose the intro, because it's not enough to be lucky. You have to work a lot around your luck.

In a song like "La Ritournelle," the B part is very surprising.

I was really lucky because I found it like that. After Tony Allen, the drum player, came. He played this fantastic part of drum and after the bass, sing and the strings. For this song, it was rare, because

"It's not enough to be lucky. You have to work a lot around your luck."

everything was natural and easy. No, the strings, it was not easy, but it was an easy song. You have to be lucky, because nobody understands the rules of the music. Why this song it's better than another we don't know, we just prefer it.

So, you have to be lucky, and it's the same with a lot of bands, it's magic when they are together. Maybe the Beatles, for example, because they are very famous. "Sgt. Pepper" it's much better than the personal album of John Lennon or McCartney, because it's magic, and we don't understand why, but it's magic. And, all the music it's like that. It's magic, and so you have to be lucky, but after [being] lucky, you have to work, because you always miss a little intro or little bridge, you know, a bridge, it's very painful in music, the bridge, it's very short, but it takes a lot of time, because usually when you go to the piano, and be lucky, you don't find the bridge. You find a chorus or a verse, but not the bridge. So bridge, well usually, I don't put the bridge in mine.

Does it feel like the main part of a song gets given to you, or are you creating it?

For me, what I really like when I am in these situations, in front of the piano, I like the harmony. I really like the wedding between the chords and the melody, and I really like when the melody [highlights] the chords. The chords I imagine with a seventh inside, you know? You have the regular chords plus you add the seventh. I like when the melody is playing and [makes a swooshing sound] you touch the seventh [makes a swooshing sound] just like that, only for one note, and I love that. That really excites me. When I do that, I really feel at the right place. I feel happy. I feel very good, and for me, when I feel this sensation, I know I'm doing something good. And, when I know what kind of chords I like, what kind of melody, I'm thinking about the lyrics, but it's after the music.

I'm wondering what a producer brings to an album. You worked with guys like Guy-Manuel from Daft Punk, Philippe Zdar.

Guy-Man was my first real experience with a producer. For "Sexuality," he really drive the — because I was full of demos, full. I had hundreds of demos and I played all these demos to Guy-Man and he chose 12 songs. And after, Guy-Man had a very clear vision of what is the best way for a song, how you can shine a song. The sound of the kick, the sound of the snares, the sound of the synth. Each chance to create something, he can bring a song [to] the best light. And I think that he did that a lot for Daft Punk. With a lot of control, a lot of maîtrise [mastery], a lot of knowledge of the production of big artists, how you can create that. All the music of Michael Jackson, Quincy Jones tricks, he knows, you know.

And so it was great for me to do it and I like that with a producer. I say, OK, I compose the song. I put some idea for arrangement, few, but now the music continues [on] your end and you're the master, you're the driver of the project. Yeah I do my own voice by myself, I have to mix my voices and blah, blah, blah, but in terms of pure music, I totally trust the producer I choose, but I choose a producer for him. I don't want to be a producer with the producer. I don't want to [be] double producer on a song. I wanted the vision of Guy-Man totally. For "Sexuality" I did all my composition, my lyrics, and I was on a big sofa watching Guy-Man doing synths or sometimes I played synths also. And it was comfortable, because he'd say, "Now we do a piano and after we do a synth, and after the synth we will do a guitar," and so you have your schedule, you know, it was easy. It's like a super quiet river to work with a producer, I really love that, but sometimes for [an album like] "L'Aventura," for example, I did not need a producer because, you know, it's just classical guitar, [with] Brazilian drums, but for electronic music, because I'm not a maker, I'm not an MPC guy or like I say, computer guy, so when I want to do electronic music, it's much better for me to be with a producer because I'm not at all a specialist of this way of music.

So you need them to help you?

Yes, if I do an album just piano and voice, of course, I can produce it myself, but if I want to do a song like for example, "Cochon Ville," I need help, because I don't know [how] to do the beat like, [makes a techno drum sound] dum, dum, dum. I can do it but that would be not very well done. That will be not perfect. That will be average. And so, I prefer to ask masters like Tony Allen for the drum, best drummer. Guy-Man, best producer. Mr. Oizo, Jam City, the English guy, high level [people], you know, who do what they do, in a perfect way.

Over your albums, you've shape-shifted to become different versions of yourself, did that come easily? Like even from "Sexuality" to "My God is Blue" it's a big shift.

I try to feel the — not the weather, but I try to feel the ambience of the society, and I say to myself, "It could be good to be this character in this society." So in 2008, it was "Sexuality." It was not at all like now, it was very bling-bling. It was champagne on the floor. It was, you know, and so I said, "Yes, I will be a French seducer, a French lover." It was cool, you know, in this bling-bling ambience to be *romantique* [romantic] but glamour. And after, I choose to be more a guy from Brazil, you know, with horses and a farm because the ambience changed. It was already more like organic food. And now I choose domesticated because it's really, you know, wash the floor, wash the windows, with the very clean society, very clean city, very clean New York, very clean Los Angeles, it's totally domesticated, so I try to feel something I hope from the world. And I try to have the good character, it's like I see the world as a movie and I give me the best role, the best character. It's not a technique, but it's a natural process, but it's also a way to choose what I want to wear. So "Sexuality," it was cool, because it's cool to have sexy clothes. It was good to have clothes of a master of sex. It's important also about your character what kind of clothes you can wear. It's direction, *et tout ça* [and all that], so it's a big ball, with a lot of *facette* [facets].

You've worked with Karl Lagerfeld and Chanel. Is working with the fashion world something that just came naturally?

For me, yes, because I like outfit. I love the texture. And for me, yes, I feel good, because it's *éphémère* [ephemeral], it's shock, you know. Something it's good, you know, but two years after, it's shitty. And I love that. You're always cleaning yourself, you're always reinventing yourself. It's very close to my process, you know? To kill the past and always be in the future. It's always a next collection, always the next step, always better. I feel a lot of relationship between me and this world because the process are quite similar in a way. And you have to feel the *tendance* [trend]. You have to feel the street. You have to feel the general ambience.

It's very close to my job and it's cool because with the new point of view, the new ambience of the world, you know, it's not good to take the plane too much, too much expensive cars full of gas, there is just a little place where everything it's still possible, you know. Gold, champagne, Rolls-Royce, it's fashion. France it's the country of luxurious brands; Chanel, Yves Saint Laurent, and so in a way, it's like a little island where it's possible to be a show-off and golden and blah, blah, blah. And so I don't want to miss this chance, because I'm in Paris, the real heart of the fashion world is in Paris. So that would be too bad to miss it, you know. It's just there. So for me, it's cool, it's again very French and

it's another world. It's something else, it's not real. It's a kind of dream or something, and I feel very comfortable like that.

I'm curious what you think of remixes of your own songs. Do you enjoy these interpretations?

It's a great sensation. Very often when I listen to a good remix of my music, I took parts of the strengths to do a stage version of the song. I remember the Midnight Juggernauts. They did a remix of "Divine," one of my songs from "Sexuality," and the remix was so good. So after I did this version of the song on stage. The Midnight Juggernauts version, and even I did a show for the TV a few weeks ago, on ARTE, the French and German TV [station]. And during this show, I played "Divine," and I played again, 10 years after, the Midnight Juggernauts version. So for me, a good remix could have a good impact on me. And I say, "Ah, OK, when I do music like that, it's also possible to do it like that." It's really important to have this window, this new point of view on your music. It's really great. And very often, remixes are a big influence on my next album, because I do an album and after that, there is, I don't know, 20 remixes. This remix could be a good [basis] for the next album, because I say, "Ah, yes, this idea. OK. When I play this chord, but with this kind of drum, OK." And that helps me a lot in my process, and remixes help me to build the future in a way.

With your albums like "Simple Minds" or "Sessions," you reinterpret your own music regularly and you find a different way of looking at it. Is that important to you, to refresh the music that you wrote a long time ago?

Yes it's really important, but first it's important for me because I go to the studio, but not to say to myself, "I have to find a new composition," it's more the composition is already done, so it's something just for the pleasure, like you know, play your song but just the piano, maybe add a little synth. And I like that because when I did "Session" or "Simple Minds," I went to the studio totally relaxed, totally without pressure, you know, it's not like, "Oh I hope the song will be good," the song already exists, so you just play it, but in a more simple version, so it's cool. And for me, the message for the audience — because at the end, records are always made for the audience — [it's that] you can really listen to my composition, it's not full of production, my music. For me it's important to show it to the audience because it's a kind of message of what is really important in my music is my notes, my chords, it's my compositions and my lyrics, and production is almost, not a guilty pleasure, but a fashion pleasure. That's the message, just listen to my songs like that, even if the next album will be full of production, it's also important to listen to my chords, my melody, it's a kind of message to say, "Don't forget I'm a composer." **R**

"To kill the past and always be in the future. It's always a next collection, always the next step, always better."

Yu Su

Shortly after leaving her hometown of Kaifeng, China, to go to university in Vancouver, Yu Su had a life-changing encounter with club culture. Already a classically trained musician, she quickly did her homework, soaking up electronic production techniques and her favorite contemporary artists, tracing their influences through Chicago house, '80s new wave, Balearic pop, and spaced-out disco. Now, not so many years later, she's had releases on PPU, Second Circle, and Ninja Tune's Technicolour label, and is also setting up her own label, bié Records. After an extensive tour of her homeland in 2019, Yu Su is shifting how she releases music, and is committed to help build a self-sustaining and internationally recognized electronic music scene in China.

Interview – Brandon Hocura
Photography – Ian Lanterman

Can you talk about growing up in Kaifeng, and what inspired your musical imagination as a child?

I always try to compare Kaifeng to a city here, but I could never really find the equivalent. It would be some kind of small town. I mean geographically small, but the population is like all of British Columbia. So it's like a very small city in the poorest province in China, right below the Yellow River. The city itself has a rich, rich history, because it used to be the capital of the Song dynasty, but you don't get an international influence like Beijing or Shanghai. So it was a pretty closed off environment. Growing up there was nothing special. It was just like growing up in a small town. But I kind of randomly got into reading magazines. There used to be a few music magazines in the early 2000s in China, and one of them focussed on rock and indie music from the West. That particular magazine only existed for maybe five years and was really hard to find. So that was sort of my introduction to Western music that wasn't mainstream pop.

Can you remember what kind of bands were in that magazine?

Well, definitely one of the first Western bands I listened to was Massive Attack and also Coldplay. So it was kind of all over the place. But nothing electronic. Back then, I didn't know what band music was, or electronic music, the difference between the genres. But I studied classical piano from 3 to 17.

So before you encountered those bands, you were already interested in music.

I was kind of forced to learn, like most Chinese kids. My mom really wanted me to get into music school and be a pianist. That was her plan for a long time. When she was pregnant with me, she listened to music all day, all night. Because she read somewhere that if you play music to a baby, you can have some kind of nice influence on them. So I wasn't against the idea, but I would say between 10 and 14 was the hardest time because you obviously, as a child, you just want to go play. No one else had to practice four hours a day. But as I grew older, I was just like, "This is nice." I was happy because it was something that I thought I could do that a lot of other kids couldn't do.

So then you moved to Vancouver for university. Why did you choose Vancouver?

My grandpa is a dentistry professor. So in the '90s, he had made trips to Australia, New Zealand, Canada, and when he came to Vancouver, I think he really liked it. When I was about to graduate from high school, my parents knew I wanted to explore more options. I think they knew that I was into music and that I couldn't really do that in the early 2000s in China, especially in my province. So they were like, "You should try to get into university elsewhere. We'll pick between Melbourne and Vancouver, because the weather is nice." And then I got into a good university in Vancouver, so they were like, "You're free to go now." So I just came by myself and started university.

How did it change your musical map when you moved to Vancouver?

I think it is all just chance. If I didn't move here, I wouldn't have gone to my first party and listened to disco music for the first time in a club.

Did it take time for you to connect with the music community or did that happen almost immediately?

I think so. I was in university trying not to fail my classes, while trying to learn English. And then I was like, OK, well I might as well try my best to find people who I can become friends with who are into the same kind of stuff, which was a bit difficult at first because of the language barrier and I didn't know anyone here.

What were you studying?

I was in business school at first, but then I switched to anthropology. I eventually got involved at the radio station at my university and I think that helped me to meet some of the people that I later became really good friends with. And then I went to [my] first party ever and that was when it all changed.

"I have no patience. I never have patience with tweaking to look for a sound."

Who was the DJ?

It was Floating Points, in 2014. It was a Love Dancing party, which were the parties that Mood Hut was doing at the beginning, before they called their parties Mood Hut. I have such a crazy vivid memory of it, even though at the time I just couldn't really understand what it was all about. Being in a dark room, all these people dancing, listening to a person playing music. Because for me, I was like, "There's nothing to see," 'cause I was like, "Oh, this is a concert or something." Everyone seemed like they were in a different mindset than me, because I also didn't know anything about drug culture. Anything. So I was like, "Whoa, this is insane." I didn't even know that all the music he was playing was old music. I thought it was modern music.

Do you remember thinking right away, "I want to do this"?

I think I did right away. I was like, how can I do something like this? How can I maybe make music like this? What is this all about? It's so fun!

A lot has happened in those six years for you.

I guess so. That's why I say it's all just coincidence, right timing. Because otherwise it just wouldn't make sense.

So what came after that? Did you start DJ'ing first or did you start composing electronic music?

I started trying. At that time everyone was all about the hardware. So when I first learned about it, I couldn't because I didn't want to just go buy an expensive thing. I didn't want to make any initial investments to try to learn something brand new. So what I did was I looked up on Google how to learn producing music for free. Then I found out about Ableton, so I torrented Ableton, and just spent a bunch of time watching YouTube tutorials. I tried asking people to teach me how to use the program, but because I didn't have the vocabulary, I just wasn't able to understand what they were saying. So the only way was to learn by myself by watching videos because you can digest things at your own pace. I would see a term in Ableton that I didn't know, so I'd look at the Chinese meaning, and then I'd look up the Chinese term, and then I'd understand it, then go back and start from there. I would do it section by section. And then I bought a keyboard or two.

Like a MIDI keyboard?

A MIDI keyboard. I was like, well, those analog setups look too complicated for me.

A keyboard is something that you already had so much knowledge of before Ableton, and it was like you were trying to translate that into the world of software.

It was just easy, because all I needed to do was plug it in because I can make a sound. If I get an analog keyboard or drum machine, I just wouldn't be able to start from a sound I like. I would have to figure out how to have a sound first. And that really influenced how I make music now. I have no patience. I never have patience with tweaking to look for a sound. I always start from having a sound that's already there and then move from that, resample things. I can't see myself ever getting into modular because that's kind of like the opposite from my instinct.

How different is your process now to when you first started? Do you think it's changed a lot?

No, it hasn't changed that much. A lot of the habits I have now come from how I was doing it when I learned. Some of the methods are not really how you're supposed to do it, but I'm just so used to that and it makes sense for me. The only difference is that now I am able to, if I have an idea in my head, "Oh, I want to make a beat that's sort of like this," I can do it right away. Now it feels easier and it feels less genre-oriented when I make music, I think.

Do you think that DJ'ing informs your production and the other way around?

I think the whole DJ thing for me is almost like me learning about the history of all these different styles of music. So it's like learning the entire thing backwards. I think if you look at the music I've made from the beginning till now, and then look at the mixes I recorded from three, four years ago till now, it's like the music I'm making is sounding more and more like band music and stuff from the '80s. Like the style of music, the sound of the music is going kind of backwards because of the new records that I keep learning about from people around me, and from digging and learning. The first record I ever bought was Beautiful Swimmers because I started from listening to contemporary dance music. I had to go backwards because I had zero knowledge of anything. I didn't even know who Laurie Anderson or Art of Noise was three years ago. But discovering those people has been changing the new music I make.

I first encountered your music through mastering that split cassette you did with CS + Kreme, that was around the same time as the PPU 12-inch. You were making dance floor music, as well as deep ambient music.

Yeah. The PPU one was at the beginning of me learning how to make electronic music. So that was kind of me doing homework. Those two tracks on the 12-inch was basically me studying other people's music, especially Beautiful Swimmers, and figuring out how to make that style.

Right. You did it well! You figured it out.

Yeah, that was me doing homework and learning, but the ambient stuff I started making at that time was just, it was natural and easy. I think from having the keyboard background.

I'm really interested in field recordings and I think you were part of a field recording project called the Pollyanna Sound Archive Prototype.
And in Vancouver there's a really long, deep history with environmental sound recordings with the World Soundscape Project. What drew you to using field recordings in your music in the first place?

Scott [Johnson Gailey] was the person who introduced me properly to what field recording is. He's done a lot of readings and he's always been interested in those things. And I can't really quite remember how or why I got into it. I think it might have something to do with studying anthropology in school because I was introduced to ethnography and lots of these research methods of documenting. And I also did an internship at the student union at my school doing archiving. So it was all these non-music related practices and the experience I've had that maybe got me into it. And just because I'm interested in this way of listening. For a while I sort of had this weird feeling with field recording because it felt like such a Western practice. Like everything, all the readings, research, the theories around field recording, it has always felt so, like, academic from this Western point of view.

Yeah. I think with the World Soundscape Project, it certainly feels like an older paradigm of field recording, and has this kind of anthropological approach to it. Do you think that you approach it in a different way?

Yeah. Because it falls so deeply in the world of sound art. I always have a problem with the world of sound art because of how hard it is to access for just regular people. I really didn't like making something more complicated than it is. And, you know, just trying to sound as obscure as you can. It's just the problem with art in general. So I would say the only difference

"You just record. Anyone can do it. It doesn't have to be this obscure research. It can just be for people to listen to the world in a different way."

I have in my approach is that I always, whenever I use field recording, I try to approach it from a more accessible point of view. And that research project I did, the purpose of it was to make the practice of field recording and listening and archiving sound accessible to everyone. Because it really is nothing special. You just record. Anyone can do it. It doesn't have to be this obscure research. It can just be for people to listen to the world in a different way. We're all hearing things every day, experiencing sound and vibration. So it really doesn't have to be this, you know, strictly "art" thing that only people who have access to this education can understand.

"So there were all these people who were basically introduced to dance music from coming to a club, thinking it's like a concert where I'm going to be playing the music that I've written."

Last year, you spent a lot of time playing and touring in China. How was that?

It was mind-blowing. It was just nothing like I expected. Ever since I moved away, I obviously lost touch with what's going on in China, and I just never really heard much of what comes out of China, like contemporary, electronic music. I didn't really hear about anything until a couple of years ago. It was so funny, because I started from just planning four dates, only four cities, because for a while, there were only like three or four major cities where there's a lot of interesting things going on. But because I had a visa issue, I had to stay in China for three months. So when I got there and played those four major cities, I started getting all these messages from people I didn't know from other cities. So I went to all these places I'd never been.

The most mind-blowing experience was playing a New Year's Eve party in this place called Xining, the capital of Qinghai province. It's next to Tibet. It's mostly Tibetan people living in that province, and there was some kind of sacred Tibetan lake that I went to that's just in the middle of nowhere in a desert. And these people got in touch. They were like, "We got a sponsorship from Absolut Vodka. They gave us some money to do a New Year's Eve party. Can we have you come play?" And I thought maybe it's not a good idea, because I was expecting in a city like that the people would only like, you know, trap, pop, hip-hop stuff. Because those things are way more popular in China. I was totally expecting to play and there would be nobody there. But it turned out that there were all these people in the Northwest areas of China, like Yunnan, who traveled to go to that party. In Yunnan, because of the rainforest, they actually have a history of trance music at parties, because there's mushrooms everywhere. People take drugs and go crazy in the tiny countryside.

So people had a great time at the party. They loved it.

Yeah. And the most interesting thing was, a lot of music I like has weird vocals or it's very Oriental or something. I like a lot of stuff that has like a Middle Eastern sound. And they were loving it so much. People were loving it

because they have a really good understanding of that kind of sound because they're all from tribes. The people there are not Han people, they're indigenous people. It was so, so strange and so great.

Were you surprised about the electronic music scene there?

Very much. In my mind at that time only Beijing, Shanghai, Chengdu, which is a lot like Amsterdam, the scene, I felt like only these places had music communities. But it turns out that it exists everywhere, which is not a surprise because if you think about how big China is and how many people there are, there's gotta be people out there, especially with [the] internet.

Do you think you'll see more DJs touring China in the future?

It's so interesting, because when I was there I think China kind of became a trendy spot for international DJs. Club Tag in China, they have like a crazy connection with Dutch German DJs, for example. When they go to Japan and Korea and Southeast Asia, they started adding dates in China, but only in those four major cities.

Right, they're not branching out.

I think it worked out for me because I'm Chinese too. So I think it was maybe easier for people outside of those major cities in China to get to know me and they see me as this Chinese person who comes from the West, but still represents China. It was like this pride thing. There were lots of young women who would come to these parties I played all over the place, and they came thinking it was a concert 'cause they got to know me through my records. They've never listened to a mix. They don't know what a dance party is. And they come and it was like me having my first party experience. So there were all these people who were basically introduced to dance music from coming to a club, thinking it's like a concert where I'm going to be playing the music that I've written. It's so interesting.

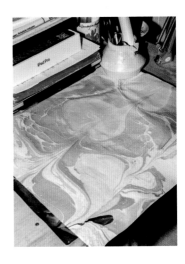

"I don't see the need of relying on outputting things from a European or UK-based source anymore. I feel like with everything in the world right now, art as well, it's so decentralized."

That's so exciting because it's like planting seeds, and to see where that will go in the next few years is pretty cool.

Yeah. And because of the pandemic and because of the fast recovery in China for the past, like three, four months, there are these parties happening everywhere, all over the place. All of these Chinese DJs were traveling all over the place in China, playing full rooms of people. Like they don't need to get these big European DJs to come anymore.

And you're going to release your record on your new label, which will be based in China.

Yeah. And we're doing the Western version with Music From Memory. That's for the vinyl. When the pandemic started, I was thinking about how I wanted to change the way I put out music, and I really want to have more things coming out of China. Things made there and that get sent to the West. Because for so long that's where the standard is always set. Like what's good music, what's bad music, what's a major label. So China was just receiving what the standard is. But I don't see the need of relying on outputting things from a European or UK-based source anymore. I feel like with everything in the world right now, art as well, it's so decentralized. I feel like it's important for me to start fresh.

Are there record plants in China?

Yeah. There's pressing plants, but I think maybe the quality control isn't as good because it's not that established. And with printing as well. That's one thing that I've been dealing with, with the people who are helping me over there is that they found the plant that can press the vinyl, but then that plant doesn't really have experience printing sleeves. They don't have experience doing all the other things. It's not like in Europe where you send the whole package and they make it. There are all these things which are really challenging right now. But I think it's a good thing to start doing. Someone has to start doing it.

Yeah. And I feel like once you figure it out, then it'll be easier. And then other people can start producing more.

Learning all the industry stuff, I now have a crazy amount of appreciation for people who run labels, like all these little things that you have to be on top of all the time.

The Knopha stuff, is that produced in China?

Yeah, He's based in China. And he's honestly my favorite DJ in China.

"You don't have to own *every* piece of gear to make something."

His productions are great too.

Yeah. So you know, the reason I want to start this label is because I'll be able to use the connections I've already made here to help good musicians like Knopha from China. Because when you're in China, if you don't get a big Western label, it's hard to get your music out there because no one is paying attention every day to like, "Oh, what's going on in China?" That Knopha record did well because first of all, it's so great. But if it wasn't a lot of people in the West talking about it with each other, it would have had a really hard time getting heard. Because you do rely on the community to receive something, right. I want to be able to build this bridge so that things can be exported from China.

I know you love food, and your Yu Su Cooks Instagram is amazing. What is the connection between food and music for you?

Well for me, food and music are the only two activities that I do every day, the only two activities that occupy my life. I think about music, and then every morning I wake up or even the night before I think, "Oh, what am I going to cook tomorrow? I want to try this new thing." Especially now that I have all this time. Because last year when I was traveling so much, I actually, I just couldn't do it. The only way that I could cook was to cook for promoters because they wanted me to make them noodles. I would go and cook them food before the party. But yeah, those things are what my life is really about. I mean, you eat, you listen to music, you think about music. I don't know if there's any particular connection between the two activities. For me, it's just like breathing air. Like there's no way I can exist for even a week without music. And with food. It's not like this extra thing, because everyone has to cook. If you have time, you have to cook for yourself no matter what you make.

Sometimes people ask me, "Can you write a recipe for this fried rice you made the other day." Or like, "You made this kimchi grilled cheese, do you have a recipe for that?" And they get no answer because I don't. I think there may be this cultural difference. Places like China, Italy, Spain, places that have a really old history of food, you don't think about cooking as [being] about a recipe. It's like the same thing with Italian grandmas making pasta. I don't have a recipe, I just put a bunch of stuff that I think will taste good together and anything can be replaced. These ingredients can always be replaced.

The same thing with me making music, because I'm not a perfectionist and I don't care. I don't have patience to particularly source the best — like every little sound has to be perfect. I care more about everything together as a result. Like nothing has to be perfect on its own, as long as it's perfect together.

So there will never be a Yu Su record that comes out with a cookbook?

Actually I started to work on a cookbook because I'm kind of under some pressure. And I think I want to make something interesting because I want to talk about this, the philosophy of cooking, to look at the activity of cooking, not as something where there's rules you have to follow. I think that's the major thing for me that I want to deliver from making a cookbook, or maybe I wouldn't even call it a cookbook, just like a little advice book, or like a handbook. It's like for example, making fried rice, you can make your fried rice with any ingredient. It doesn't matter.

In our house we call it "leftover fried rice" because it'll taste delicious with whatever you had for dinner the night before.

And there are all these things that you can replace. I was just talking about this with a friend the other night because someone called me when they went to T&T [Supermarket], and he said, "Can you just tell me all the sauces I need to have at home? Like what do you have?" So I gave him a list of like basically 10 things that I always have at home all the time. You can use certain sauces and ingredients from different cultures to still make the same thing. Like you can make it a paella with Chinese flavors. It doesn't matter. So yeah, I think it's time for me to write a recipe book about how you don't have to follow a recipe. [*laughs*]

But you're right. It's like music though. That's how music evolves.

Yeah. Like if you don't have a Juno, you go to YouTube and look up like a Juno demo and you just sample the sound from that. That's what I've been doing. You don't have to own every piece of gear to make something. I don't have anything at home right now. I went from buying a lot of gear, to now I don't really use anything. I sold my last keyboard, the last piece of gear I own the other day. It all comes down to how you approach it. If you just want to make music, you can make it with anything. **R**

Gerd Janson

Starting out writing music reviews was Gerd Janson's pragmatic way of having a job connected with the dance floor. To him, being a working DJ just didn't seem like a valid career option. But what began as a side hustle blossomed, and before long, Janson found himself not only DJ'ing as a career, but launching his Running Back record label, while his calendar of gigs continued to fill up, reflecting not only Janson's success, but his indefatigable work ethic that makes it very hard for him to say no.

Interview – Karl Henkell
Photography – Nils Müller

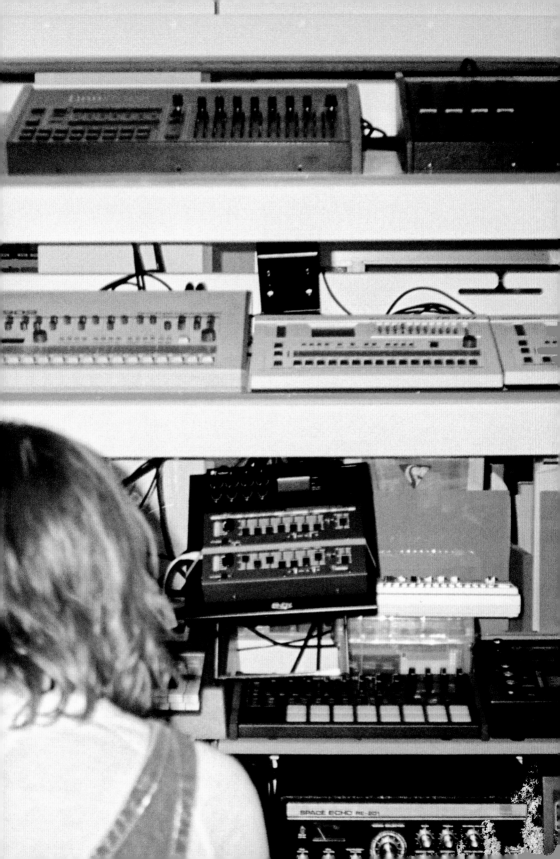

"I liked DJ culture from the get-go, although I never wanted to be a DJ."

How did it start for you? I read about you as a boy scout discovering a tape?

I liked music from a very young age. Like even as a 5 or 6-year-old kid, I just liked listening to music. But with my parents not being known for their refined taste in music, it was more like what I saw on TV or heard on the radio. But like really, even when I was doing homework, I always had the radio on, you know. I was already into music, and then we went on this now-legendary boy scout trip and one of the leaders had this Sven Väth club night tape. One of these guys had like a tape of a club night, and we were in a pink Volkswagen bus going on a hiking trip and listening to this tape and this music sounded so different, you know, and it was like unheard stuff. And it was more wild even back then, you know, the one track I remember from that tape and I always quoted is a Homeboy a Hippie and a Funki Dredd's "Total Confusion," where you have this hip-hop thing, and then the rave steps. And it was just like total madness. And then the guy told me, yeah, "We go to the Omen." And so in my head, it was this utopia, you know, like, and even from that day on, I went to concerts and stuff, but I always liked secondhand music, played from a system, you know? Because you have the recording and it's been tailored to the occasion. I liked DJ culture from the get-go, although I never wanted to be a DJ. I was happy to be on the dance floor.

Was Sven Väth a household name at that point, or was he kind of obscure?

He had this kind of pop star career as a singer from OFF. "Electrica Salsa" was also like a big Ibiza record or just a big dance record. I mean, if you look it up, you'll find it immediately. But for me, being like 12 or 13 at the time, OFF's "Electrica Salsa" wasn't on the menu. You know, I think back then, because you didn't have the internet to go back, even like one or two years, everything people say, "Oh, everything is so fast these days." But I think back then it was even faster, because if you didn't catch the bus, the next bus was coming, but you didn't know what was on the last, you know? Now you can look up the bus plan. Does it make sense as an analogy?

I know what you mean.

In 1992, when I started going out you had no idea about what was being played there. You know, it was all hearsay. And I think that's why a lot of scenes were, or are still nowadays so interesting to look back at because they were local. When you went to Mannheim, club culture was totally different than in Frankfurt. And even if certain records were being played in both places, it was really different, like a different way of dressing, different DJs playing the music in a different way, yeah?

But going back to your question, if Sven Väth was a household name, I think he was. He was already the guy back then that a teenager like me knew, this is like the cool techno DJ. You know, or like the one at the schoolyard, people were like whispering his name: "*Sven Väth.*"

Was that all before your time going out to clubs?

I was like heavily underage, so I was relying on older friends and their friends to kind of take me under their wings and sneak me in. A few times I also had to stay outside because, I mean, I looked very young. I think if I take the beard off now, I still would look — I mean, maybe all the late nights now took their toll, but back then, you know, there was no way that you would think, "This guy's older than he looks," you know.

And you had to be 18 to go to a club?

Yeah. I mean, there were some places where you could get in with 16, but then you had to leave at midnight. Of course, you know, you couldn't drink hard alcohol or whatever, which never interested me in those surroundings anyway, I wanted to go for the music and dance. And I danced for hours. Like in all those places when I got in. Actually, the Omen, I think I only went twice. In '93, I think I was still 15 when I went the first time. Which is like pretty young. But the first time I went to a rave, I think I was 13. My mum drove me there. But it wasn't in a regular club, it was more like a rave, a party set up on top of a swimming pool area.

"This kind of epiphany on a dance floor, lights on the DJ. 'Oh I wanna be the Pope.' I never had that."

How would you have found out about it?

Friends again. They were like, "There's this party, let's go." And I'm like "Oh, can I come?" "Yeah, come on, we'll take you." So that was basically a way because raves didn't have that [security presence], especially the illegal ones. I mean, of course, they had an eye that it's not full of kids, you know, but they weren't like — in the clubs the bouncers were really checking IDs.

And there was even the way of faking your ID with like the custom roll from a cigarette pack, because it looked kind of the same. So you had to find the right number to fake your birth year, or your birthday. And then it worked. And that's why a lot of bouncers, they had this move with the thumb to go over your birthday. I never faked it myself. I got in because my friends knew the bouncers at that point. So you were just like, not trying to stand there too long.

Did you have a big brother who helped?

No, I have a younger brother, he's one year younger. And actually I remember, one time, there's this club in Mannheim, Milk, which is also kind of an important place for the history of drum & bass, jungle music in Germany, and he got in and they asked me for the ID. So he always looked older. It was more older friends. But it was basically something, at one point everyone I knew was into it. Like even the people who weren't into it, they were into it because it was kind of a youth culture phenomenon, it was a fun thing to do. Not everyone started to get as nerdy about it as I did.

But it was in the air?

Yeah, it was in the air. You went there, you know.

Is that because of where you are in Germany? Like if you grew up elsewhere that might not have happened as readily?

Yeah and I mean, I was born in Romania in a German village, and I think if my parents would have stayed there, I don't know if we would be here now. That thing as a youth culture movement always had that part of taking part in it, you know? Do something, do a party, clothing label. It was this kind of DIY spirit. I think that's where it's kind of comparable to punk, you know, that you thought with the tools you had at hand, you could do something. Like a sort of empowerment. But I thought the only thing I could add or contribute was

writing, because I liked to talk or to read and to write. So I thought, "OK, this is maybe something I could do." You often read interviews with people and they're like, "Yeah, the first time I went to a party and I saw this, I knew I wanted to do this," you know, like this kind of epiphany on a dance floor, lights on the DJ. "Oh I wanna be the Pope." I never had that. And at that time it was, except for Sven Väth and maybe a few others, it was more like you had hundreds of DJs who were just the guys in the corner. So I think, that was really the point where it was different to the rock & roll band image, you know, where you had this kind of sender and receiver thing, both facing each other, you know, it was more like, the dance floor was a bit more of a loose thing, you know?

The DJ in the corner.

And a DJ was in the corner and of course he had to see what's going on. But I still remember the first time where it really flipped in the early 2000s, where you really could see not only the "deck sharks" as we called them, you know, the people like me wanting to see what the record is, or like guys who wanted to, you know, if someone like Jeff Mills played, you always had like this trough of guys who wanted to see the actual technical skill of what people did, or were able to do back then. And then it changed that like this whole dance floor was just directed to the DJ booth, you know? And I still, to this day, I find it rather unpleasant that they watch you doing that thing, you know?

Why do you think it happened? To make it more sellable?

No I think it wasn't that people decided that, "OK, we have to make it more sellable now." I think it is just like a dynamic that happened from the dance floor rather, that DJs became even more cult figures than they had been maybe to some people early on. And they wanted to see, you know, instead of going to a club because you know that club was serving that type of music and you could only hear it there, you go now to see a DJ like you would go and see a band. And I think that happened, you know?

Did it have anything to do with mobile phones having cameras in them and people wanting to take photos?

That's another thing I remember when I saw it the first time at the Time Warp, a rave in Mannheim, and I think it was the first time Richie Hawtin started to do his Plastikman live show again. And it was this sea of people with a phone, that's where I saw it really in one unison move. That's where I was like, "OK, this is changing." But it's a bit like the chicken and the egg thing, you know? All of those people wouldn't have come with an analog camera to take a picture back then, but because they have a phone that has this ability to take a picture, you start to use it, you know.

So back then you decided to go the writing route. You were saying there were like a hundred DJs in the corner, was there the feeling that a lot of people were lining up wanting to DJ?

No, I mean, you had a lot of people collecting records and being like bedroom DJs and maybe also thinking or wanting to play, but I think it was never, like, a valid career option back then. That's why I also never thought, "OK, I could learn this and then travel the world."

> "I started it from this kind of fan thing, you know, 'Oh, yeah, let's make a record.' But then, at one point you realize OK, for some people, it's not only a fan thing, it's their livelihood"

And so you started writing for Groove. Were they in Frankfurt at the time?

They were in Frankfurt. They came from this local fanzine, Frontpage, which is another big German techno rave magazine. It also came from Frankfurt, but Frontpage started as a derivative from like Dorian Gray and the so-called "techno nights" there and electronic body music. So it was like a fanzine concentrated on that.

Groove was more like dance music in a broader sense. So you could find, like an interview with a local hip-hop DJ or act there, and the next page you had like a house thing, and then techno, and it just slowly evolved into this kind of techno rave magazine, you know?

And then, Frontpage moved to Berlin pretty early on. I think because the founder, Jürgen Laarmann, saw the potential and the difference, you know, while in Frankfurt, everything happened in clubs and discotheques. In Berlin, of course, you had clubs and discotheques, too, but you had this kind of abandoned building thing where they always make up this Detroit-Berlin connection because I think in that sense, they were really similar that you had all these abandoned places where you could do something, and Frankfurt is a banking city, so you don't really find many abandoned buildings where you can just set up a sound system and go, you know?

So there was this move from Frankfurt to Berlin?

Yeah, but I think Laarmann was really early on doing that. And it took another 10 years almost until it became the "it" thing to do.

I think the first and one of the only times I really applied for a job was I sent my application to Groove magazine because they were looking for writers and they even called me back which was kind of...

And was that to work in the office, or—

No, it was like writing reviews and stuff like that. I think they called me back because they recognized me from my picture, because the guys saw me at the parties all the time. So I think that was more [the reason] than my meager writing skills that they thought, "OK, this guy's there the whole time."

At the same time I started to DJ, but just because by then I had built a record collection, and Thomas [Hammann] used to have a record shop in Darmstadt [called Pentagon] and he was the local hero DJ at a place called Café Kesselhaus and he saw us always coming in and he liked what we were buying, not everything I guess, [laughs] but like in general he thought, you know, OK, cool kids. And, so we got the opportunity to DJ there.

It seems like there's lots of record label distributors and an industry around that in Offenbach and Frankfurt?

Yeah, there used to be at least three, four or five distribution companies. I mean, even a student town like Darmstadt, at one point, they had like, I think three to four record shops that were designated DJ record shops, you know. One guy was more drum & bass and jungle, and one shop was maybe a bit more trance-y or whatever. But like all of them had a variety of stuff, and it catered to people who were looking for dance music in one way, shape, or form. And then you had maybe the same amount of normal record shops, you know. But of course over the years, it died down. I think there is no DJ record shop there anymore because times just change, but it was at that time, it was like a very healthy environment, you know, and you drove 30 minutes to the next town, and you had the same thing, you know, so you had to put the miles in, but you had access to stuff.

So at that point, you weren't thinking about pressing a record?

No, it's the same as with becoming a DJ, I never really thought, "OK, I need to do this label." It was just like, while I was already DJ'ing for a few years — or not too many years, like maybe three, four — I had friends making music, and you know, if you're new and starting out, even if you like established things, but you also have the feeling of leaving your own mark or doing things differently, and I think that is important for the whole thing, also to stay fresh, to have new people coming up who you know, come from a different corner or another angle and do their own thing. So I tried to do that. At first, the idea was like, it's for all my friends who make music, and were too shy to send off their music to existing labels, or did stuff that wouldn't fit in there, and in the beginning, I also thought, "Oh maybe it would be a good way to reissue records." Even back then, you know, but mostly records you couldn't get your hands on. So, you know, for myself to actually have them.

When did you start Running Back Records?

I think the first record came out in 2001. And I was still at university and it was by no way a thing with a business plan or even a release plan, you know.

It was like one or two records a year. The friend I started it with, Thorsten Scheu, he stopped actually producing electronic music and went more and more into like Northern Soul territory. I was not that interested in that, at least not enough to make a side branch of it. Other guys stopped being interested in [producing electronic music] as well. So I started to look for music by people I never met personally. And also to start slowly to work like a real label, but I would say it took at least another five years until I had the feeling, "OK, this is a label now," you know. And maybe another three or four years until it clicked with me, "OK, this is not just pressing a few records, selling them, giving the artists some money." You have to make it more serious if you really want to keep on doing it, because then you have a back catalogue. You have some responsibility for the artists, you know, it's not just like this — I mean I started it from this kind of fan thing, you know, "Oh, yeah, let's make a record." But then, at one point you realize OK, for some people, it's not only a fan thing, it's their livelihood, you know. So you need to try and make the best you can for them also. Then you need to get a label manager at one point when you DJ so much that you can't go through Excel sheets on a plane anymore.

"I think it's actually a very privileged position to be able to be annoyed by dance music."

Do you ever get to a point where like, you can't listen to dance music anymore? Maybe at home you don't listen to it?

I mean you have to put the hours in to find new stuff, but that's why I say passion profession, when you start doing it, you go down to your basement DJ booth, you know, and you play records for hours and just for your own entertainment. That's what I maybe mean with an overdose, you know and it doesn't mean I hate it, but if you do this three times a week in a environment with people, you don't come home on a Monday evening or a Tuesday and then go to your record basement to be like, "Oh yeah!" Maybe if you're like in your early 20s, but yeah. And there is also other stuff in life, you know, riding a bike, going for a walk.

But hey, on the other hand, I come from a working-class background, so this is maybe why I always did everything that I was allowed to do. With this kind of, like, "Yeah, I do everything. Yeah, I do it, I do it, I do it." Yes man. But also at the same time this kind of, I would've never thought I end up here, you know.

You wouldn't have thought it went this far.

It wasn't the plan. I would've thought when I started at university, OK I'm finished with, even with German standards, 28. And then I work as a journalist somewhere or even I do an academic career, I stay at university and have this normal, settled lifestyle. Go out dancing once in a while or so. So, I don't want to sound like, "Oh, it's a terrible place, nightclubs! Oh I can't stand it anymore," you know. I think it's actually a very privileged position to be able to be annoyed by dance music.

In your DJ'ing life pre-COVID you are usually traveling a hell of a lot, does it feel like you are working for it? It's not like the income all comes from one mega stadium event or something.

No, I was playing a lot. There is always this kind of, "Oh, I don't get paid for playing, I get paid for traveling," which I think is kind of not true because you would want to get paid even if it's in your town, you know? But what that sentence is maybe supposed to mean, the DJ as martyr, it's like this, "Oh, yeah, I'll die for you people," which is, of course, like I said, even if it has its downsides, it's still a privilege. I mean, you get paid to see the world one time, you know.

But if you do it in a frequency that I did it in, which is of course also my own doing, you can always say no, that's what I maybe meant [by] working-class. It's hard to say no if you think, "OK, this might go as soon as it came."

That is definitely the hard part of it, this kind of traveling, lack of sleep. Even if the hotels are nice, those are hotels. You are in this constant state of flux or stress; come from one thing, go to the next thing. When you're at the party playing, that's actually the point where it kind of all then makes sense, even as corny as this sounds, you know, then that's OK. That's the nice moment, and of course, the nice dinners you have with people and stuff. But sometimes when you take one flight, another flight, a third flight to get somewhere and the environmental issue put to the side, although it would be way worse for the environment if everyone that saw me play would come to my place, you know. So, yeah, it takes its toll.

Have you ever thought I'll do this for X amount of years and then scale it back?

I mean, I would have never thought that I turn up in my 40s with headphones still, you know, to a club, but I still do it. So, my thing was always, "I will stop when I'm 50." 50 sounds great, you know and it's still, you go into retirement. I don't know. Like as long as I think "the young youth," as Gregory Isaacs might say, would want to see me there, I might be doing it. But I can't see myself playing up to 200 gigs a year at 50, you know.

What was the maximum amount of gigs you played in a year?

I think between 160 and 180, something like that. It basically went up every year.

It's an exciting thing as well, I suppose for you?

It becomes almost like a challenge in sports. You know, like if you ever used to run for a while, you try to become, "How much more can I take, you know?" Or like, I don't know, weightlifting, you know.

Can I lift some more.

Yeah, can I lift some more, and I always said I'd do as much as I can until I know what too much is.

"There is also other stuff in life, you know,
riding a bike, going for a walk."

"I think you can have both. You can know about the past, but you can still try to live for the future"

Do you know what too much is?

I think now I know it. [*laughs*] I got pretty close to it.

Are there still milestones that you want to hit or places to play? Or is it more just being in the flow of DJ'ing constantly that's interesting for you?

Yeah, I think it became the flow kind of thing, you know, that you had like — I'm not overtly nostalgic, so to me it's more about, I mean, which sounds weird for someone that studied history and collects old stuff, you know.

Who has part of Tony Humphries' record collection upstairs.

[*Laughs*] Yeah, but, I think you can have both. You can know about the past, but you can still try to live for the future instead of trying to recreate things that in your mind were like this, you know. I'm sure there were people who frowned about all the legends of today. I remember when I started going out there were always people even back then telling you, "It used to be better." I think that's also like basic human psychology.

It was better in 1920 than it was in 1928.

Yeah, yeah, I think that is the main problem. And then you even have young people with that state of mind that they wish themselves back to a faraway place in the past.

Do you feel like your generation was part of that?

No, I remember like DJs back then, before I was DJ'ing saying, "Oh, yeah, this record is already two weeks old, you can't play it anymore," you know. So, it was very much about the future. And then I would say maybe in the late '90s with the internet, where you could finally access a Ron Hardy mixtape actually, you know, and Tony Humphries radio shows and a Warehouse tape from Frankie Knuckles, where you could actually hear for yourself what you only read about. Then it made you yearn for it a little bit more, you know. And you tried to incorporate that into what you were doing as a DJ, because you learned more about it, so you saw, "OK, I can also program it like this."

I also learned from just watching other DJs playing, the way they touched the records or the pitch. I remember the first time I saw, I think it was Joe Claussell, just using the pitch on the Technics to ride a record, you know, like make it faster, slower. And the German kind of techno DJ or even the European thing was more you touched the platter and then you corrected the pitch and you always used both hands and the Americans, most of them, at least those from the New York type of school — Chicago, Detroit, is a little bit different again — but they let it go and then it was only surfing the pitch.

To make it line up?

Yeah, and I tried to learn it for myself because it was so unusual to me that I wanted to crack the code of how to do it. And I found it this way, it's easier to mix records that have a loose rhythm grid.

Is there less to see now where people are using CDJs rather than turntables?

I don't know, I like to think if you're a young person getting into this and the first time you walk into a place, like, just for the lack of another place that everyone knows, Berghain, which is like this cathedral thing. I think it still knocks you out of your shoes. The way I was knocked out of my shoes when I saw David Fascher who was like a Hamburg turntablist guy doing scratches on turntables, live the first time. He was like this kind of body scratcher, using elbows and stuff, but he was dressed fly, he had a nice windbreaker, which is maybe weird to compare those things, but I think you can still get excited by it. And I think for people, yeah, maybe they just look on YouTube tutorials of how to do it.

There's something about going to where it happened.

And I still think that's what I also thought back then. You can put in all the hours you want, collecting music and trying to make sense of all of it and the technicalities of it, but if you wanna be a DJ I think you still have to put the hours into actually doing it in front of people, you know. All theory is gray, you know? You have to get a feel for it.

I would never say I mastered anything … I have this impostor syndrome with it, because I still can't believe that I actually do this for a living. **R**

Record

June Jones

After fronting Melbourne's beloved heavy-folk trio
Two Steps on the Water, June Jones put down
the guitar and taught herself to play the keyboard,
and produced her debut album, "Diana." Avoiding
the trappings of nostalgia, Jones's love of sci-fi —
particularly its world-building focus — has informed
her songwriting, as she aims to write music that
sounds like it could only be made in the present,
which June argues is a kind of sci-fi in itself.

Interview – Kiloran Hiscock
Photography – Patricia Casten

Did you teach yourself to produce?

Yep, about 10 years ago I had a friend who taught me a little bit of Ableton and I had some rough things I was doing back then. But I didn't start it again until two years ago and then the last two years has been writing the album, learning how to use Ableton, producing the album and mixing it myself.

Do you find that having those skills to self-produce helps you bring your vision to life more effectively?

I'm quite particular about what I like, and I don't know, maybe I'm overconfident with my belief that I can figure out how to do stuff myself, but I did have a particular vision for this record and what I made is the vision combined with the reality of what I was capable of, so the eventual product is something in between, which is always the case. With art, I have this big vision and then I have the reality and what funding I have or don't have and what instruments and software and tools and expertise I do or don't have.

That's like a lot of creative things, it's never quite what you imagine, and the reality of it is different, but that can be good. Stuff comes out that you wouldn't expect.

I've always had a very strong DIY ethic, and it's interesting because I feel some of the sounds I'm engaging with and styles of music I'm borrowing from are less rooted in DIY ethics, and it's interesting trying to make a synth that sounds like a synth on like a Robyn record, but doing it on a pirated version of Ableton on a tiny refurbished office laptop. It's a frustrating reality but it's so funny that I don't mind.

When you say DIY ethics, are you talking more about punk music?

Yeah, which is where I started in high school, I was in a lot of bad punk bands. And music that didn't require high-fidelity production.

What were those songs about in high school?

I wasn't really writing the lyrics in high school, I started as a drummer for a couple of years and then I started playing guitar and I only really started writing lyrics towards the end of high school. I had a band called the Twisted Ankles and I think we played like, five shows. It's interesting because these days I value songwriting and lyrics very highly, but at that time I think I was someone who didn't really listen to music for the lyrics and I think that really shows, because my favorite band at the time was Pavement. We had a lot of songs about nothing.

These days, do you normally start with the lyrics or the music? Or does it depend?

More often than not I start with the lyrics. And then I'll try and write it with some chords on piano and find a good melody, but there have been times where I try

and do something I don't normally do, like find a synth loop and build a song around that. And I think that often does result in different songs, but on the record they've been songs that have been more challenging for me to get to a place that I'm happy with.

Why do you think that is?

I just have a method that I'm quite comfortable with, and, doing things outside of that feels important so I can challenge myself to not do the same thing. It often feels a bit more like walking in the dark and feeling around, and trying to make something via a process that I'm still learning.

Does "Leafcutter" have a thematic core?

It's funny, if it has a thematic core now it's probably closer to what I'm more comfortable with and accustomed to, than what the record was going to be. There was a period where I was trying to write more on a macro level and to explore the context of my experience, whereas often what I'm writing is the experience itself. And I was trying to reflect on a broader sense of hopelessness and apocalypse, but I just realized that that's not really my strong suit, and where I do feel comfortable and where I feel like I have a practice is in more self-reflective and "confessional" songwriting. I think there was a period where I felt like maybe it would be somehow better to not write confessionally in a way, feeling like it was naff or uncool or maybe even narcissistic or something, but the more I worked on this record and explored sounds that are more electronic, I began to feel like it was exciting to make a confessional record using sounds that are more associated with abstract, broader ideas. So I came back to my comfort zone and that's more what the record is now, it's more another record about me. Not that people need that.

A lot of music is confessional, but so many genres or types of musicians don't get labelled as such, and it's interesting to think about why that is.

It makes me think about how we accuse some people of being emotional as opposed to logical and then you look at all of these people who are supposedly the logical ones and you can see how deeply in their emotions they are, and how emotionally informed their viewpoints are.

I feel hesitant to call myself a confessional songwriter and the term singer/songwriter is very loaded. I have this sense that people associate me with folk music because of the band I was in that used folk instruments and had folk influences. What I'm interested in now is aesthetically quite far from folk music, but I also want to feel comfortable in the fact that a lot of my songwriting has been informed by folk music and folk music-adjacent genres, because that's often where I've found the richest lyric writing.

"It's interesting trying to make a synth that sounds like a synth on like a Robyn record, but doing it on a pirated version of Ableton on a tiny refurbished office laptop."

Who are your songwriting influences?

It's funny, I've only ever really been able to pinpoint one where I can really see how much that's influenced me, and that's John Darnielle of the Mountain Goats, who is a songwriter I came across when I was maybe 17? It just felt like a new kind of way of thinking about the world in those lyrics that really resonated with me at that time. A lot of that songwriting is not the emotions in their rawest state, it's kind of like one step back and a self-awareness in the way that they're being presented, someone who's feeling a lot but also able to thoughtfully express those feelings.

And I guess that's where I was at for a large period of my life; I was feeling very fucked up, and so it was really exciting for me to find music that was expressing that. And I think that's a lot of what Two Steps on the Water was for me, a project of processing trauma through those songs, and the solo project feels like it's coming from a less emotionally raw place, maybe.

You can hear that in your different vocal style as well, compared to your solo work.

Yeah, like I just found that I wasn't writing songs that demanded a screaming crescendo at the end of the album, I feel like I'm a lot calmer these days. I still find myself inside very all-encompassing emotions, but in a way that feels like I can also get out of them and look at them and write about them as opposed to writing from inside of them all the time.

There is a quote about the song "Jenny (Breathe)" from your upcoming album being about "surviving inner trauma and outer dystopia." Is that a theme you set out to explore?

I wasn't planning to do that, I had a vision for the sounds I wanted to work with and musical influences in terms of a sound aesthetic, and just kind of let myself write however I write in terms of lyrics. There was a time when I was trying to zoom outside of my experience. Part of the original idea was I wanted to make something that felt really big and less like one person's life, but have since come back to my inevitable curse of being a confessional songwriter.

"Some people talk about peaking in high school and I feel like, either I haven't peaked, or I peaked in year 6."

Do you think anyone has ever successfully done that?

Good question. I'm sure people have. I think that idea came from reconnecting with this lifelong fact of being a nerd and loving speculative fiction, particularly science fiction, which is often about world-building and establishing the world that the events take place in. So, I was like, how would I do that in the context of songwriting? And I gave it a whirl but it wasn't as good as I wanted it to be. I think my hope is that the world-building aspect of this album will come through more from the instrumentation and that will establish an atmosphere that surrounds the literal lyrics. My original idea was — there's this term "space opera" which kind of refers to things like "Star Wars" and "Dune," which are not even my favorite kind of science fiction, but I think I just love this idea of a space opera. One of my favorite movies as a kid was "The Fifth Element," which has a literal opera scene in it with this blue alien woman, it's amazing. I wanted to make something super dramatic and futuristic, while also recognizing that the future from science fiction is also the present that we live in.

What do you love about science fiction?

I think part of it is just a sentimental attachment 'cause it's something that I've felt connected to since I was 10 years old and watched "The Matrix" for the first time, and some of the video games I played as a kid, like "StarCraft." I was into "Warhammer" in primary school but it's kind of an inaccessible game because you have to have so many figurines, and they are so expensive, so I didn't play the game that much, I just loved the aesthetic.

Did you ever get into Dungeons and Dragons?

Yeah, I've played D&D as an adult and that was really fun, and I'd like to do more of that in the future. I'm quite into trying to let go of self-consciousness around being a nerd. There's a certain kind of person that pivots between being a nerd and having latent theater kid energy and I think I was really in denial about both of those things as a teenager because I was like, oh all I care about is punk and music.

As if they were at odds with each other.

Exactly. I actually did acting classes in year 5 and 6 and then I got really into punk in a very annoying way. I remember quitting acting classes because it felt like it really clashed with my sense of self as this fucking 12-year-old prepubescent punk. Which is quite tragic because it was one of the best things as a kid. I was the lead in our year 6 play that was written by our drama teacher. I played a character called Blaze and I don't remember anything about the play and I'm so sad no one has it on VHS because I think that some people talk about peaking in high school and I feel like, either I haven't peaked, or I peaked in year 6. I'm not sure if I'll ever get back to the glory of Blaze.

What kind of science fiction do you like?

Ultimately, I like the kind of science fiction that isn't what people think of when they think of sci-fi. When people think of science fiction, they think that the most important thing in those stories is the ideas and hypothetical situations, and I love that as a backdrop, but I also really need something that feels like a human story inside of it. I love Ursula K. Le Guin, and this year I've been reading some Octavia Butler. I read "Parable of the Sower" and a book of short stories called "Bloodchild," both of which were amazing and absolutely devastating. I read a truly amazing book called "An Unkindness of Ghosts" by Rivers Solomon. It's an amazing book that deals with ideas that are very real here and now; ideas of gender, neurodivergence, race, and class. I can't say exactly why I am more drawn to these stories within the context of science fiction, but I think science fiction does allow for such broad expansive imagination. I enjoy the play between reality and hypothetical.

"In life I'm always trying to find the balance between being poisoned by irony and overly earnest."

Sometimes I feel like there's almost not enough acknowledgement of how much we live in sci-fi present, and sometimes I feel a bit like — it feels strange sometimes to make something that feels like it could have been made fifty years ago, or even twenty years ago, because the world is very different. And I think that was part of my desire to engage with sounds that feel more current and future-looking. And I don't know if I've achieved that all the time. But I did have a moment after making "Diana" where I felt like, I felt an aversion to nostalgia and nostalgia informing new art. I felt a discomfort with making music that inadvertently idealized the past, and was almost pretending that things are like they were when they're not. And so part of the idea for the new record was to make something that felt more honest about where I'm at and where we're at and what's possible and what's real now. Recognizing there are things from the past that are great but that doesn't mean we have to do them again.

Nostalgia is everywhere and it's a thing that's always existed, but it feels like the gap is closing, films we grew up with are already being remade. I wonder why we're all looking for this comfort? Maybe it's stopping us from moving forward in some way because there's such an obsession with it.

Totally, I really think — I'm not trying to be a conspiracy theorist, but I think that nostalgia serves a function within capitalism, it serves the function of distraction from things that are happening, and it also helps us convince ourselves that there is an eternal truth to life. What I mean is nostalgia is a warm and comfortable place to be, and it really serves a purpose, and it's important to have those things, I guess I don't want to make something like that again.

The idea of dystopia and apocalyptic themes are really present in popular culture and discourse at the moment. Do you feel like there's a responsibility for artists to respond to these increasingly dystopian times?

What you're saying is important to remember, dystopia feels like it's arriving for some people but there's been apocalypses before. People like me who are white and

middle class are for the first time feeling that maybe our apocalypse is coming too. It's really important to not erase the fact that apocalypses have been happening as long as colonization has been happening and longer, and it's not as simple as "the end of the world" for everybody because we all have little worlds inside the big one. I don't explore it because I feel like I have a moral duty to anything, I guess it affects me on a deep emotional level. And that's a lot of what informs my songwriting is my emotions and my emotions feel very tied to what has felt like for our generation, we grew up with apocalypse media and climate change as this very real and irreversible result of capitalism. It's been something that has been on my mind since I was about 10. And I remember watching "BTN" ["Behind the News"] in primary school and hearing about the drought, and witnessing all these unprecedented years of bushfires and hurricanes, and I just don't know what it would be like not feeling like that. I've been thinking about the end of the world since I was a kid, so it doesn't feel like an external thing I'm reflecting on, it feels deeply tied to my internal world.

You have a blend of wry humor and candid poignance which really hits me in the gut. Humor is something people often use to deflect or avoid, but in your lyrics, it feels really honest and deepens the impact. Does that come out naturally in your songwriting process?

Sometimes it's been conscious because I haven't wanted to make music that was only sad. I really enjoy the combination of sadness and humor, tragedy and comedy, and crying and laughing. Sadness and humor really complement each other. Sometimes I feel like if I'm writing a really tragic song it's the place where I'd most want to put something funny. To provide relief in the feeling but also acknowledge that often things that are very sad are also a little bit funny, or maybe that they need to be funny and we need to make jokes that are quite dark. In life I'm always trying to find the balance between being poisoned by irony and overly earnest. I don't feel comfortable being wholly in one camp.

When there's something funny followed by a line that really hits you, it makes it more impactful. I'm thinking especially of the lyrics in "Look At You Go."

That's funny because that song came about really suddenly and I slapped it together in a way, and it has a pretty sort of minimalistic production, but it's also one of the only songs that got a Spotify playlist and has considerably more listens than any of my other songs on Spotify which is sadly a reflection of, something. It's a funny song, but something I really regret about that song is that one of the lyrics refers to the year 2018 as the present, which is what it was when I wrote it, but when I released it, it was 2019 and I was like, "Fuck, this is committing some kind of crime. As a songwriter I've done something profoundly bad." But it's immediately followed by a reference to eating arse so it gets eclipsed by a bigger more important topic.

I'm interested in these characters, these Meryls, Dianas, Jennys. What's it all about?

The name of the last album, "Diana," is my middle name that I gave myself in honor of my grandma Diana. She was my father's mother who I did not know very well but she was quite an amazing woman on paper. She was a farmer, radio host, communist, and feminist at a time when that was less acceptable. A lot of "Diana" feels like a reflection of an experience of mental illness, and she is someone who the family speaks about as a forebear of mental illness and neurodivergence in my family, which is full of those things. I didn't really know her, but she feels important to me. As someone who has struggled to place myself in any kind of lineage, whether it's in my family or being a white settler in Australia and feeling conflicted about how much I want to have tradition, which tradition feels important. And as a trans woman who chooses her own name, I could choose anything, but I still felt compelled to connect myself in that way that people often do with their children. They give them the name of a grandparent or great-grandparent. I kind of did that with myself with Diana. And that has an analogue in the way that I make music because there are some traditional elements of songwriting within the tradition of pop music and folk music songwriting in the West in the English language that I don't feel the need to throw away, so I'm always trying to find traditions that I want to keep and combining those with elements that are newer and don't have such a history.

And Meryl is kind of a pun, because the character is a mayor, and mayoral is the adjective. There's this part of me which is like, I've been a middle-aged white woman since the day I was born. Meryl, Diana, June all feel like old women drinking tea and using foul language, and that resonates with me. And the first song on the new record is "Jenny" and I don't even really remember why that name came about. But that song is also writing to myself, and Jenny and June are very similar names. I was tempted to call the album "Jenny" and have a through-line of albums named after women.

Do you have a name for the new album?

It's called "Leafcutter," which is a name I settled on after a long series of trying to find a name for the album. "Diana" came quickly and instantly fit, and because this album has changed shape so many times it's had lots of different working titles in my mind. There was a real moment where I was like, "I think I'm going to call this album 'A Bug's Life.'" I love the movie "A Bug's Life," it was one of my favorite movies as a kid and actually a great piece of socialist propaganda and it takes its story from one of my favorite movies as a teenager, "Seven Samurai." It's basically the same story. I was deeply agoraphobic as a teenager and ended up spending a lot of my time being very pretentious in my interest in movies. I have a collection of interviews with Akira Kurosawa that I've never read but have owned for over 10 years.

I don't remember the film but I do remember I saw it several times. I didn't even bother with "Antz."

"Antz" is fucked. "Antz" is bizarro "A Bug's Life." They both have voice actors in them that are absolutely terrible people. But I had a long period where I was looking for a name for the album that spoke to the themes of the record and my girlfriend, who listened to the record a few times pointed out to me that there's a lot of themes of being underground and underwater and this sense of being "under" things. There's also a couple of references to bugs. I'm quite into the idea of the butterfly as this cliché symbol of transness and reclaiming something that's so cliché and a bit naff. I was thinking about different words and everything I came up with seemed too sterile and scientific and then I settled on "Leafcutter." I'm not trying to make too direct an analogy with it but there's a leafcutter ant and a leafcutter bee and I just liked that it was almost this adjective before these different insects but also referred to a relationship with nature, one in which there's using of tools and affecting nature and being affected by it. It's a theme that comes up in my music sometimes, a theme of trying to understand my own relationship to nature as someone who grew up in the suburbs, but also quite close to the city with parents who do not fuck with nature; no camping trips, very little street smarts for camping. I love the humble ant. Don't relate hugely to the ant because I feel ants are extremely hard working and very community-minded, but maybe I aspire to be like the ant but in reality, I am a mere human. **R**

Postcards Through Time and Space

If you asked listeners of Beats in Space — the radio show Tim Sweeney's hosted for the past 21 years on WNYU — what physical ephemera they associate with the show, chances are they'd say the Polaroids of each week's guests. But there's another physical piece of the show: the postcards sent in from listeners around the world. With Sweeney ending the show in March 2021, we've put together a selection of postcards sent to the show's final address, the Weinstein Dormitory at 5-11 University Place, as a tactile memento of many years on the airwaves.

Artwork supplied by Tim Sweeney

ROMA
Piazza San Pietro
Place Saint Pierre
St. Peter's Square
Der Petersplatz

A kiss from the
pope for over
1000 heavenly mixes!
I'll go to heaven or
HELL as long as they
have BEATS IN SPACE

Beats In Space
c/o WNYU
5-11 University Pl Basement
NY NY
           10003
            USA

I wish I had some
hundred-dollar bills
to throw at Panorama
Bar last Sunday.
You gave us our
money's worth!

Best,
Anthony

LUFTPOST
PAR AVION PRIORITAIRE

JAHRE WWF
Natur schützen: wwf.de

50 Jahre Fehmarnsundbrücke

Deutschland

Beats In Space
c/o WNYU
5-11 University Pl.
New York, NY 10003
USA

Pablo Picasso (1881-1973)
Tanzende Silene   1933
Gouache und Tusche   34 x 45 cm
Die Sammlung Berggruen in den Staatlichen Museen zu Berlin
© VG Bild-Kunst, Bonn 2003   Nr. 1164

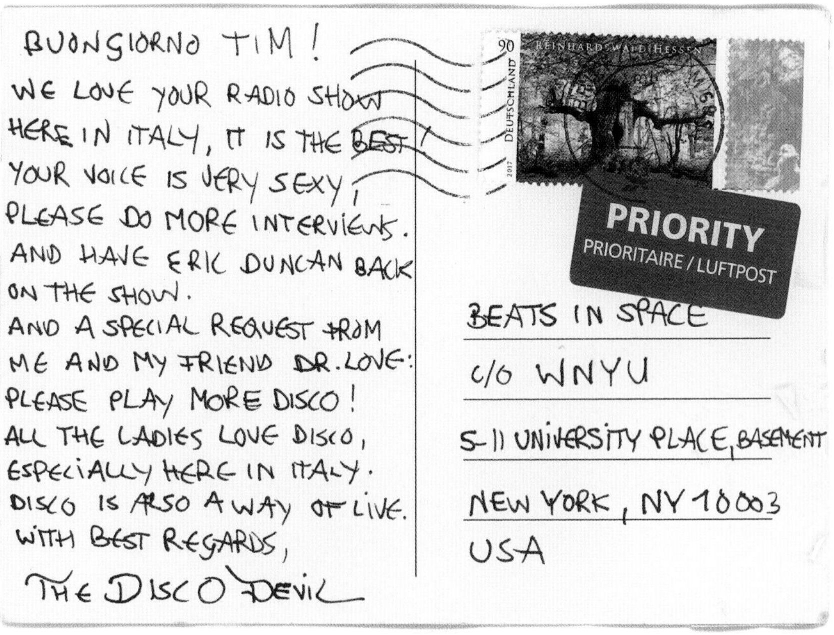

BUONGIORNO TIM!
WE LOVE YOUR RADIO SHOW
HERE IN ITALY, IT IS THE BEST!
YOUR VOICE IS VERY SEXY,
PLEASE DO MORE INTERVIEWS.
AND HAVE ERIC DUNCAN BACK
ON THE SHOW.
AND A SPECIAL REQUEST FROM
ME AND MY FRIEND DR. LOVE:
PLEASE PLAY MORE DISCO!
ALL THE LADIES LOVE DISCO,
ESPECIALLY HERE IN ITALY.
DISCO IS ALSO A WAY OF LIVE.
WITH BEST REGARDS,

THE DISCO DEVIL

BEATS IN SPACE
C/O WNYU
5-11 UNIVERSITY PLACE, BASEMENT
NEW YORK, NY 10003
USA

90
REINHARDSWALD HESSEN
DEUTSCHLAND
2017
PRIORITY
PRIORITAIRE / LUFTPOST

BUONGIORNO TIM !
WE STILL LOVE YOUR SHOW AND WATCHED
IT CLOSELY, BUT THERE WAS NOT ENOUGH
DISCO MUSIC. WHY? WHY?
DUE TO THIS FACT AND WORLDWIDE
IMPORTANCE OF YOUR SHOW, THE WDAC
(WORLD DISCO AFFAIRS COUNCIL) IS
HOLDING EMERGENCY MEETING IN A TOP
SECRET LOCATION IN EUROPE NEXT MONTH.
I'M A MEMBER TOO AND I WILL LET YOU
KNOW ABOUT THE OUTCOME OF THIS
CONFERENCE. HOLD TIGHT !
YOURS TRUELY
                THE DISCO DEVIL
PS: PLEASE BRING BACK ERIC DUNCAN !
PS 2: OR MORGAN GEIST, HE IS DISCO TOO!
PS 3: HOW IS BATHHOUSE SCENE IN NYC?
PS4: DISCO IS A WAY OF LIFE AND YOU
     CAN DO IT TOO, TIM ♡
PS 5: DR. LOVE MADE THE ARTWORK ON
      THE BACKSIDE. YOU CAN ALSO BUY
      IT IN DISCO ART GALLERY IN ROME !

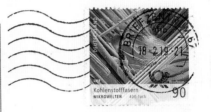

BEATS IN SPACE
c/o WNYU
S-11 UNIVERSITY PLACE, BASEMENT
NEW YORK, NY 10003
USA

BEATS IN SPACE c/o WNYU
5-11 UNIVERSITY PL, BA5
NEW YORK, NY
10003

GATEWAY TO FAIRYLAND — New Market, Va. HAND COLORED
Jless Caverns POST CARD

Here two huge stalagmites, overhung with
numerous stalactites varie-shades
ues, form the gate-way to Nature's Underground fairyland the diminutive Palace of
the Fairies and the exquisite little jewel
almond Lake.

SWEET CORN FOREVER USA

Hi Tim !!!!!!

Thanks for the
hundreds of mixes!!
I've been listening for
years and will listen
for years to come!
Lookin forward to
majic touch!
XOXO -Aaron Rodriguez

Beats In Space
C/o WNYU
5-11 University Pl.
Basement
NY NY 10003

POST CARD

NEW YORK
20 MAR '19
PM

Thanks for all the
amazing mixes!!!

A01 Jafta Cards, Harare, Zimbabwe

U.S. POSTAGE
$.34

11211
Date of sale
12/26/17
06   2S00
08341084   SSK

Tim Sweeney
Beats in Space
C/O WNYU
5-M University Pl
Basement
NY NY
10003

Nelson Mandela, Hon Doctor of Laws,
University of Zimbabwe - June 1986   (Photo: Alexander Joe)

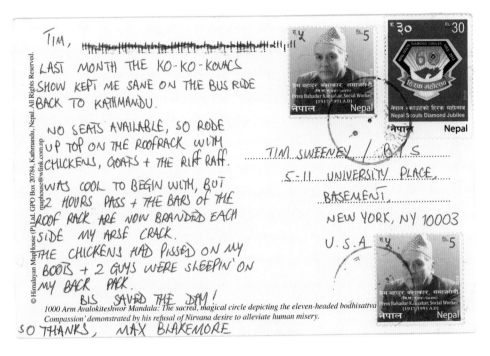

TIM,

LAST MONTH THE KO-KO-KOVACS
SHOW KEPT ME SANE ON THE BUS RIDE
BACK TO KATHMANDU.

NO SEATS AVAILABLE, SO RODE
UP TOP ON THE ROOFRACK WITH
CHICKENS, GOATS + THE RIFF RAFF.

WAS COOL TO BEGIN WITH, BUT
2 HOURS PASS + THE BARS OF THE
ROOF RACK ARE NOW BRANDED EACH
SIDE MY ARSE CRACK.

THE CHICKENS HAD PISSED ON MY
BOOTS + 2 GUYS WERE SLEEPIN' ON
MY BACK PACK.

BIS SAVED THE DAY!

SO THANKS, MAX BLAKEMORE

TIM SWEENEY / BIS
5-11 UNIVERSITY PLACE
BASEMENT
NEW YORK, NY 10003
U.S.A

1000 Arm Avalokiteshwor Mandala: The sacred, magical circle depicting the eleven-headed bodhisattva Compassion' demonstrated by his refusal of Nirvana desire to alleviate human misery.

Sunrise #8
The magical world of the desert begins with the first
morning glow of the rising sun. Daytime animals begin to
stir from their rest, it is time for the night creatures to
scurry to their burrows. Life here in Joshua Tree National
Park is determined by the daily cycle of the sun.

LOS ANGELES CA 900

2017 PM S L

Photo by Buster L. Wright © Photo Works, Joshua Tree, CA 92252

Mississippi
FOREVER/USA 1817

dynacolor
graphics, inc.®

Tim,

DROVE thru Joshua tree
last week, listening
to stallions mix.
A Perfect moment.
LOVE you + BIS!
-LUCAS

Post Card

Beats in Space
C/O W NYU
5-11 University Pl.
BASEMENT, NYNY
10003

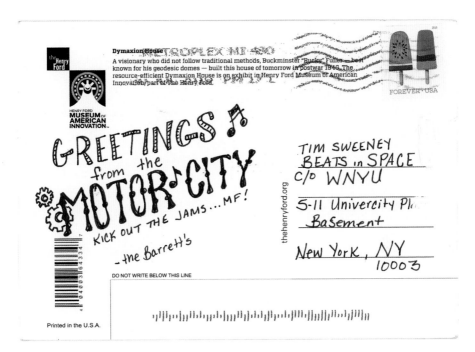

Dymaxion House

A visionary who did not follow traditional methods, Buckminster "Bucky" Fuller — best known for his geodesic domes — built this house of tomorrow in postwar 1946. The resource-efficient Dymaxion House is on exhibit in Henry Ford Museum of American Innovation, part of The Henry Ford.

FOREVER USA

the Henry Ford

HENRY FORD
MUSEUM of
AMERICAN
INNOVATION.

GREETINGS
from the
MOTOR CITY
KICK OUT THE JAMS...MF!
— the Barrett's

thehenryford.org

TIM SWEENEY
BEATS in SPACE
c/o WNYU

5-11 Univercity Pl
Basement

New York, NY
10003

DO NOT WRITE BELOW THIS LINE

Printed in the U.S.A.

The Twilite Tone

The Twilite Tone may have only recently released his debut solo LP, "The Clearing," but the man behind the moniker, Anthony Khan, has been at it for 30 years. First hooking up with Common — before he was known as Common — and No I.D. as CDR in the late '80s, Khan has worked in the studio with the likes of Gorillaz, John Legend, and Kanye West, picking up Grammy nominations along the way. Now, he's taking all of those experiences, and creating new music that's very much his own.

Interview – Bruce Tantum
Photography – Lyndon French

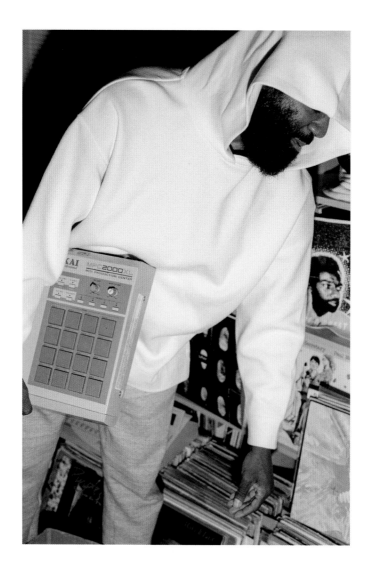

"Most parents are like, 'You need to stay in.' My mother would say, 'You need to go out to dance.'"

Do you feel there's a through-line that runs from the music you were making three decades ago to the music you are making now?

I do. And this album helps to articulate it in a deliberate way. That's another reason why I wanted to make this record. I mean, I don't want to start with nostalgia; I don't want to start with "Mercy," I don't want to start with Gorillaz. I do want to start with where I am now. This is me. The album doesn't say Kanye West, and it doesn't say Damon Albarn. But hearing this record, you can quickly identify the through-line with my work before this point. For instance, I used the drums from the first single we did with Common ["Take It EZ"] on the second track on the "The Clearing" ["The Lite"]. That's an example of a common thread right there!

How did the album end up on Stones Throw? The label feels like such a perfect fit for it.

I had spoken with Chris [Manak, Stones Throw Records founder, aka Peanut Butter Wolf] in passing a few times. There were some projects they wanted me to produce on, like Steve Arrington and such. But what brought this together, specifically, is that I was out here to DJ with a friend, Dave Mata [from Chicago's Soul Summit party] who actually was meeting with Chris, and he invited me to come hang out with them. We were just talking casually, and Chris asked me what I was up to. I told him, "Well, I've just finished an album," and he said, "I'd love to hear it!" I played it for him, and by the time it was over, he was interested in putting it out. I'd always been thinking about Stones Throw, it was probably in my top three, and I'm happy to have it as a platform.

"Do It Properly," with those heavy beats and bassline, has a really unique feel. Can you talk about how that track came together?

Those drums, I was just really crunching them up. It was all done in the MPC 2000XL. I didn't run it through a plugin or anything. The [Khalid Muhammad] sample that's in there, that was actually the last thing that was added to the song. I use that soundbite when I DJ. He's talking about colonialism and slavery and all the things that have been taken from us as a people in that process. But I changed the context of it.

In what way?

To mean, let's let go of all this, so we can come to a clear space and be free. I'm certainly not arguing with his viewpoint, I agree with it. But I'm in another space where I really think knowledge is time-based, and we need to let go of some knowledge. I find it very interesting that we, as humans, make things holy just because it's written in the book. But written by who? And when? What was influencing them? Why should I think this is gospel? So that's why I used that speech at the top of "Do It Properly." The song is about standing on your authentic self. If you are authentic in what you do, then by default, you do it properly.

I composed "Do It Properly" while I was living in Crown Heights, Brooklyn. I had just broken up with my girlfriend. Well, one of the breakups. We broke up three or four times. [laughs] I spent that day working on that music, and it just kept growing and evolving. I don't even think of it as a song, it's more like a suite. It's just transcendent.

It sounds like you enjoy that song as much as I do.

You know, my favorite music is the music I make. I'm deliberately playing notes and chords that are resonating with me, and resonating from me. "Do It Properly," even though it's instrumental, is very meaningful and poignant, both the music and the song's video.

That video, with you dancing your way through various Chicago locales, is pretty amazing as well. You have a background as a dancer, right?

Definitely. My parents are dancers and I've been dancing since I was a kid. Most parents are like, "You need to stay in." My mother would say, "You need to go out to dance." She was encouraging me, as a young teenager, to go out to parties! It's just something I do.

That video was directed by my life partner, Christine Ciszczon. She's a photographer, but her eye is such that she could direct motion pictures. I came up with the concept with Christine and one of my best friends, Rob English, not to show [how] great a dancer I was or anything, but just as a way to express freedom in real time. I have a personal connection with all of those places where I'm dancing. They all were pivotal places at pivotal times in my life, and what I'm really appreciative of is that the video affected a lot of people emotionally, without me having to use words to explain that.

"I've never had any lessons or anything — nothing like piano lessons — music is just wired in my DNA, I guess."

The video for the album closer "Taxi Cab Confessions," on the other hand, feels more literal.

When you go on a journey, you might end up testifying to what you are going through to someone you don't know. And by the end of it, you are free. You are home. That's what's going on in the video. This lady doesn't know me when she gets in my car, but she's compelled to share what's going on with her. By the time she gets out of the car, she feels lighter.

The song itself came about when I had to do a gig at the Water Taxi Beach [a long-defunct outdoor venue in Long Island City, Queens]. I come from the school in Chicago where DJs — Li'l Louis, Ron Hardy, Frankie Knuckles, Gene Hunt, people like that — would be playing original, unreleased tracks in their sets, either tracks that they made or tracks that kids had given to them that nobody else had. The rawer it was, the better. I would make tracks when I was DJ'ing in New York just to play out, to have something new, and I literally had just thrown this track together. The response was incredible.

You had mentioned the MPC earlier. You go with a pretty stripped-down studio setup, right?

Very stripped down, not a lot of bells and whistles. I try to do intricate things with simple instruments. The MPC is the center of my production, both technically and for the sonics of it. It just sounds great. It enables me to just get to it, rather than navigate through a lot of technology.

Sometimes the simple ways are the best.

I do love new technology, but I feel like I have to be careful of having shiny eyes around new gear. I mean, think about it: bass, guitar, drums, and piano have been used for hundreds of years, and you can still get so much just out of that. You can do straight-ahead jazz, or you can do post-punk. You can do anything! It's the same with my simple, stripped-down setup. It's not limiting, because I'm not limited. That's why I refuse to categorize myself within a genre; I'm categorizing myself as "trans-genre."

When you sit down in front of your MPC, do you have a pretty good idea of where you're going to end up, or do you prefer to see where it takes you?

The latter. I like to fool around! [*laughs*] Even when I have a deliberate idea beforehand, the process ends up being experimental. Making music is about throwing colors on the wall, and shaping it from there. And a lot of it stems from whatever's the stimuli before I walk in the room, or even when I'm in the room. I'll play a record, I'll like the drums, and decide that I want to chop those drums up and see what I can do. I'll use something that's been used millions of times before, but how can I do something new with it? How can I mess with the approach? The goal is to come up with something that I feel is me, that's what I want to say.

You said earlier that you don't like to start with nostalgia, and I know you like to look forward...

Yeah, I look forward so I don't run into anything!

But let's talk about what's led up to this moment. You grew up near New Orleans, right?

I was actually born in Chicago, but I moved to southeast Louisiana when I was around five. I was back and forth a couple of times. I went back to Chicago in junior high school, and then finally again [in] my sophomore year in Chicago.

What are your earliest memories of music?

Man, that's kind of like, "When did you take your first breath? Do you remember when you first inhaled?" It's always been a part of my life and lifestyle. I could speak at an early age, and one of the things I could do would be to listen to the radio, and be able to recite what the Top 10 was. It was uncanny, my mother would actually gather people around for that. I can also remember my mother giving us Walkmans, and I'd try to hook them together to DJ with. I'd take them apart and figure out how to do pitch control with them. I'd always be the one to fix the stereo, too. No one ever showed me how to do it. I just knew what to do.

Sometimes I'd gather my brothers around the stereo for us to sing Earth, Wind & Fire songs, I'd be singing "Fantasy" or something, and I'd be crying because it touched me so much. My brothers would be like, "What wrong with you?" I'd say "It's Philip Bailey, and he's talking about Exodus!" They go, "Can we just play some football?" [*laughs*] I've never had any lessons or anything — nothing like piano lessons — music is just wired in my DNA, I guess.

"I'm an artist. I've always been an artist. But for a long time, I kept it in the closet."

That might be true. Besides your parents being dancers, your uncle is the bassist Hassan Khan, who's played with the Five Stairsteps, the Staple Singers, Eddie Kendricks and tons of other notables.

Yeah, he's definitely done some things. He married Chaka Khan, too. That's how she's Khan. And my cousin is the jazz and classical double bassist Richard Davis, who's played with all of the greats. He's a great himself. So maybe the fruit doesn't fall far from the tree. It's both nature and nurture.

As a teenager, weren't you kind of straddling Chicago's hip-hop and dance music scenes?

Because of our time in southeast Louisiana, we were privy to what was going on in the rest of the country, and that was rap music. When something came out in New York, which is where most rap music was coming from then, Louisiana had it. But once we were in Chicago, those parties my mother was making me go to were Chicago club parties. The music didn't have a name yet. Some people were saying "house" and some people weren't. But it was that scene, and I guess I was in the second generation of that, or maybe the third.

At the same time in Chicago, we were fortunate to have college radio stations like WHPK and WNUR that played hardcore rap. The term "hardcore" hadn't been misappropriated yet, it basically meant underground hip-hop back then. It just meant music that was closer to how it was when it was just two turntables and somebody keeping the break of the record going. That's what hardcore still means to me. It was later, with the onslaught of West Coast rap or gangster rap, they started calling that hardcore. Anyway, all the while I was going to those parties, my brother was listening to these college radio stations, and that kept me in it. And that's what gave me this dual life.

The rap and club scenes were quite separate, right?

They were fully anti each other! You'd hang out with this gang, and then you'd hang out with that gang. Once I had my own gang that was into both scenes, we'd go over here and they'd be like, "Oh, you guys are ghetto hip-hop guys." And then with the hip-hop guys, it would be like "You guys are gay." We were an island unto ourselves. It was a real civil war, and we were the warriors. Fortunately, I had met friends from different sides of town who I could be in community with, otherwise it would have been super lonely. The way we dressed, the way we danced, it was the culmination of these so-called genres that supposedly didn't work with each other. Being exposed to Ron Hardy and Frankie Knuckles, and Red Alert and Bambaataa, and later, Kid Capri and early Funkmaster Flex, along with industrial and punk and post-punk and a lot of other things, that was us. You know, when De La Soul and A Tribe Called Quest and Jungle Brothers came along, I thought they were from Chicago.

Why is that?

Because they were coming from a point of view that we were coming from. They weren't like other rap artists; they were sampling dance records! When A Tribe Called Quest sampled "Running Away" by Roy Ayers, I was actually mad. I was already sampling that! I'd be in a room experimenting with these different tones and textures thinking, how I could make them go together, how can I make this work? It's not a formula, like OK, now I'm gonna add dance music to rap. It was just the natural order of things, through my way of being.

What first led you into DJ'ing and production?

Like a lot of people in Chicago, I got into it through dancing. Everybody used to dance to Ron Hardy and Frankie Knuckles, and some of those guys went on to become the greatest DJs. Dancing is such a big part of it. Like, I'm not a flat-footed DJ; I'm dancing when I DJ.

It was dancing and DJ'ing, together, that inspired the production. It's what led me to want to produce original content. I wanted to be able to say more, either in addition to the records I was playing, or maybe even opposed to that. It all worked together and works together.

How did you first hook up with Common Sense and No I.D.?

I was singing in a group that was making dance music at the time. They had a group, too, and they had a session after one of our sessions. This was in a friend's basement. They were called CDR. This guy Corey, Dion aka No I.D., and Rashid aka Common. They looked like rap, with their Adidas suits and their b-boy stance. I was like, "Oh, these guys are rappers? OK, I'm gonna hang around!" My hair was crazy back then, I was punked out, and basically looked like somebody from the dance scene. They laughed, but they said, "Aren't you a DJ? Alright, let's do an audition." A week later we did that audition at another friend's house, I DJ'ed for them, and they went crazy. And that's how I became their DJ.

Do you still have all your old records? And are you still a vinyl guy?

Oh my God, how could you even ask such a sacrilegious question! [*laughs*] I do and I am. People call me up just to tell me they have new records in, and will open up their doors with just me in there to shop. I go to estate sales, I go to thrift stores. I love records. Records are so much more than just the sonics coming off the vinyl. It's the aesthetics, just looking at the artwork, learning who played what on this, who engineered it and everything. Records are the gift that keeps on giving.

Anyway, we were a crew, but we were all working on separate projects as well. I was working on Rashid's demo, and he said, "Hey man, I'm gonna call myself Common Sense. What do you think?" I said, "I think that's awesome!" And that's how he became Common Sense. Dion, meanwhile, was using some name that I hated, so I told him, "You should call yourself No I.D." That's how long I've known those guys.

Later on, around '91, we got picked to come out to the New Music Seminar, and Common got his "Unsigned Hype" in the Source, and then there was a deal, and we were working on an album, and the rest is history.

After all of your success with Common, you stepped away from production after that for a while. Why was that?

Well, I was disheartened with the way my music career had been going with the gentlemen we just spoke about. So I fell into the role of superstar DJ, which was a great hustle. I could do that without having to try too hard, and I could stay in the limelight.

From the way you say that, I'm guessing it wasn't all that satisfying.

I'm an artist. I've always been an artist. But for a long time, I kept it in the closet. I didn't even come out as an artist to my parents until this album came out. [*laughs*] But seriously, it was satisfying financially and in an ego-y way, but ultimately it felt like I was selling out. My soul was not being fulfilled. That lasted for way longer than it probably should have, but it did teach me some lessons.

Such as?

To stop hustling my gifts. That's what I was doing from the mid '90s on till 2000. I was hustling a little after that too, but by then, at least I was hustling with music that I wanted to play and that I really liked. I started being on the underground scene, going to things like the Winter Music Conference and South by Southwest, and going to New York and playing at places like APT. The Suite 903 world, the Fader world — it was great. I also started putting out the kind of music that I wanted to, independently and on the underground. And that's pretty much led to where I'm at now.

I was just listening to that "Mean Machine" EP you did that came out on UNO. It's some pretty tripped-out stuff.

Yeah, and that's my sound! Someone has to be a quote-unquote "head" to know about that record.

Sometime during this period, you were living in New York, right?

Yeah, I lived in New York for maybe around 10 years. I was there because my good friend and colleague Duane Harriott had brought me out to DJ. Duane is incredible. I guess the term would have been he's an

> "I needed New York. I needed to be around real peers, as opposed to people posing as peers, or posing as friends. I needed the stimuli of the city."

encyclopedia of music, but now I guess you'd say he's a Google of music. [*laughs*] I was actually planning on moving to LA at the time, but not long after hanging with Duane for a bit, I moved to New York instead. It was hard because I was going through a separation from my ex-wife, the mother of my two sons, but it was so necessary. I'm so proud of myself that I was able to do that, because if I hadn't I probably would not be speaking with you, there probably wouldn't have been an album. A lot of stuff wouldn't have happened.

It sounds as though the move was probably like a clearing of its own, in a way.

I needed New York. I needed to be around real peers, as opposed to people posing as peers, or posing as friends. I needed the stimuli of the city; I needed to be amongst the giants, and the ghosts of giants. I needed to be reminded that I am a giant, and of what kind of giant I am.

"The best piece of equipment that I have is my point of reference."

At some point, even though you had rediscovered your underground side, you started working with some pretty big names, people like Kanye and John Legend. Did you seek out those people?

Nope. It's just that I'm blessed with relationships, and with a reputation that precedes me. With Kanye, I was in Park City, Utah for a surprise birthday for Common, and Kanye was there. We're both from Chicago, so he knew who I was. At some point, I had my headphones on, making a folder of disco songs I was going to edit to play when I was back in New York, and the headphone accidentally came out. He heard it and said "Man, what is that?" I told him it was just some records that I was editing, and he said, "Man, if you have any soul samples, we're working on a new album." I was just like "OK, cool" or whatever, but I could vividly hear my mother's voice in the back of my head, saying "Fool, stop what you're doing and play Kanye some of your music!"

Smart mom.

Yeah! So I said to Kanye, "Yo, check this out," and started playing him music that I was making. He was like, "What the hell is this?" I told him it was my music, and then he played me "Mercy" in its embryonic stage. It was just the trap thing with the 808. I said, "Well, it's cool. But I expect more from you." I think he was like, "What?" Because I was so forthright. A week later, when I was back in New York, he had me come to the studio where he was, and I started working with him. By default, after working with him, I started working with John Legend and Pusha T and Big Sean.

Work was coming to you.

Yes, but then I had a valley where nothing was going on. I'm not an industry guy — I don't have relationships with A&Rs, I don't have beat compilations, none of that — so I'm thinking, what do I do next? I was laying on the floor, like "Fear and Loathing" in New York. But then I get a call from an A&R at Parlophone Records, saying that Damon Albarn is interested in working with me on a new Gorillaz album. I got on a Skype call with Damon, and we hit it off, and they flew me out to London. I was supposed to be out there for a week, but then they wanted me for two weeks, then they wanted me for a month, and then I was there for the rest of the year. So like that, the work just manifests. And I've realized that my DAW is my mind. The best piece of equipment that I have is my point of reference. That's why I'm in those rooms. **R**

Eug

Plenty of DJs have another day job, but not many
have one on the same level as Eugene Whang.
Since graduating from design school in Vancouver
in the late '90s, Whang's been an industrial designer
at Apple in San Francisco. He can't say much about
that side of his life — "there's only so much I can
talk about" is Whang's go-to response when asked
about it — but as it happens, his love for good design
also plays into Public Release, the record label
he's been running for the last decade-plus, as well
as in his parties and collaborations.

Interview – Bruce Tantum
Photography – Ulysses Ortega

Were you into music when you were young, any more than the average kid?

Looking back at it, maybe, though I never really thought about it that much. There was always music on at home — classical music. Then I got into the kind of rock that all the other kids were into, and when the electro and breakdancing thing was taking off, that was on my radar. By early high school, I was basically listening to a mix of things — Jesus and Mary Chain, OMD, rap and rave stuff. When I began to DJ later in high school, I started off with hip-hop and rap.

Did I read somewhere that you studied violin as a child?

My parents got me into that, not only for musical reasons but maybe for disciplinary reasons — learn something, stick with it, that kind of immigrant Asian parent mindset. This was when I was in elementary school.

Were you already interested in design at that age?

I was really into design from a very early age. My father is an artist and a sculptor, and he was into all kinds of things like Japanese ceramics, English pottery and certain kinds of painting, and people like Henry Moore, so it was always around. He'd also do graphics work on the side for friends. That all seeped in. Then in high school, I had a really great teacher who had a class called Communication Design, which is essentially kind of graphics. They had a few Macs and I was learning to futz around with them. It all blossomed from there.

Was there any idea at that age that either music or design would become your life's focus?

Music never really seemed like a viable job. It was just an ethereal thing that was always out there, like water or air, and the people who produced music were like demigods. So no, it never felt like a viable career. But design, on the other hand, was more tangible. There's a real practicality to it. The DJ'ing was more for my own enjoyment.

It was strictly vinyl at that point, right?

Yeah. I was initially playing mainly hip-hop, so I was buying a lot of that. I'd just play these little events — friends' house parties and stuff like that. But there was also a great store in Vancouver called Odyssey Imports, which had a lot of stuff from the UK and Europe. I would hit them up for all my house, techno, and rave. I was rolling with a crew that was strictly rap, so I was keeping that stuff pretty quiet; I was buying them more just for myself. At the same time, I was just beginning to discover magazines like DJ Mag, and I would look through them religiously; I would really follow the charts to see what people were playing. I was also getting into things like the Face and i-D, pretty much anything that was covering UK fashion, art, and design.

Record stores were a great way to develop your taste. There weren't necessarily listening booths — there would be a turntable at the checkout, you'd stand in line with your stack of records, they'd play them, and the whole store would be hearing them. Which made you really careful about what you were choosing, because you wouldn't want a stack of really bad records to be playing. It can be an intimidating experience, and a kind of rite of passage. It really helps to tune your radar.

Were you DJ'ing much by the time you were attending design school?

Well, I actually didn't get into design school right away after high school. I didn't get accepted, which was pretty disappointing, so I took a year or two off while doing part-time at a community college. But I skipped half of the classes and just played a lot of basketball.

You've had a lifelong love of basketball, right?

Yeah, I've been playing basketball since I was really little. It's one of the avenues that got me into rap and hip-hop and that whole culture. Anyway, I was DJ'ing a bit at the time — mostly playing records at friends' houses — but I was buying a whole lot of records. I was friends with a lot of people who were producing music, and friends who were rapping and breakdancing and doing graffiti; it was just what we did. Eventually, I did squeak into design school, and started studying industrial design.

You had mentioned the practicality of design before, and it feels like industrial design is a particularly practical subset of design.

I think I've always been into industrial design. When I was quite young, like still in elementary school, I was into drawing stereo componentry. I remember my parents helping me mail a sketch of a receiver and a tape deck to Toshiba. It wasn't even addressed to a specific person, just to the company. That kind of thing just seemed normal to me.

It's always amazing to me that so few people are really aware of what industrial design even is. It's everything you touch, every single thing. Like I said, my father is a sculptor, and I find that industrial design and sculpture are very similar, but they have very different practical outcomes. Sculpture and art are meant to bring about an emotional response; there's an emotional problem that's being solved. When you bring sculpture into the design world, you end up with industrial design, which is meant to solve a different kind of problem.

Once you got seriously into your industrial design studies, did you still have time for music?

I was still buying a lot of records and playing at parties. It was a part of my life. By then, I was playing all the UK stuff, and through that I was discovering the Chicago and Detroit stuff.

"Music never really seemed like a viable job. It was just an ethereal thing that was always out there, like water or air"

After you graduated, how was it that you ended up at Apple?

There were a few companies that I really respected and admired, and Apple was one of those companies. Since I was playing a lot of basketball, I really appreciated what Nike was doing as well, but I thought Steve Jobs was an absolute genius, and I could really get behind what he was trying to do.

How Apple actually happened was that in my final year of studying industrial design, I needed to get an industry mentor. At the time, Graphis had published the "AppleDesign" book, and in the back of the book they had photos of the Apple designers — there were maybe only 10 of them back then. I saw a photo of Jony Ive, who later became my boss, and I saw one of another guy, Danny Coster, who is this cheery Kiwi surfer dude. I got a good vibe from that photo. I knew that if I contacted Jony, I probably wouldn't be able to get through, so I figured I'd try Danny. I guessed at some email addresses and sent him an email, and I also cold-called him and left a message.

And that actually worked?

I did get a reply: "Hey, thanks for getting in touch. Yes, I may be able to be your industry mentor."

Cold calling actually works!

Cold calling was never a weird thing for me. I was just like, "Oh, there's a phone number, let's call it and see." It was like when I sent those drawings to Toshiba. That kind of attitude has carried on and really helped me.

So that's how I got in touch with Apple. Then at the end of that year — I think this was around when the iMac had just come out — they were looking to bolster the team, and they let me know that they were looking for someone just out of school to join the team. I flew down to Cupertino a couple of times and interviewed, and it worked out.

You were working under Jony Ive, who's something of a demigod in the design world. As a young guy fresh out of school, was that intimidating?

Very intimidating! All of those guys, I was intimidated by all of them, really. But they made me feel at home very quickly, and they became my brothers. I can't say much about the work process, but it's a very collaborative situation.

Soon after you got that job, you were living in San Francisco. Did you know anybody in the music scene there?

No one at all. But when I first got there, around '99, I was in so over my head with work, anyway. There was immense pressure at Apple. There were so many times that I wouldn't know the lingo and would just nod my head, and would spend the night trying to catch up and figure out what was going on. There was no time to even entertain the idea of DJ'ing for the first few years I was there. But I had brought my turntables down with me, and when I got my first real paycheck, I finally bought 1200s, and I was making some mixes at home.

What had you been spinning with before?

I had weird ones, Technics 150s. They had digital pitch control, and thankfully were direct drives. I still have one of them in a closet, it's kind of a meaningful object for me. Even earlier, I had been using turntables with belt drives, which were impossible to do anything with. But at least that taught me how to touch the records properly.

Finally, sometime around '04 or '05, I started a night with a friend called Weekend. The music was like mid-tempo house with a little bit of downtempo, and we'd mix in a little bit of rap and funk. It was Friday monthly at a tiny dive bar in the Tenderloin called Julip, which was not part of the circuit at all. That was my first party here in San Francisco.

Was there any ambition of playing in actual clubs at that point?

Well, we had a few different sets of friends. Some of them liked going to the clubs, and I enjoyed that too, mainly for the sonic experience. But we had a lot of friends who preferred to hang out at dive bars, and San Francisco has a lot of great dive bars. The goal was to get a bit of a club vibe in a dive bar.

In 2007, I started a party called FACE with my friend Justin Montag. Justin was from New York and had come from the Fader magazine; he now does Franchise, which is a great basketball magazine. We were doing it in another dive bar in the Mission called Amnesia. It was more like an indie bar, we were the first night they had where people were gonna be dancing and getting wild. That was when we first started bringing people in to play.

> "I'm used to caring about the whole package, which is something that I think I learned from working at Apple, where we take care of every micron."

But it seems like you did take those parties fairly seriously. You were already paying a lot of attention to things like flyer design, for instance.

Yeah, the flyers for Amnesia were kind of divey and rough and raw. We did have a lot of fun with the design and the aesthetic of the whole thing. I've actually always cared about every aspect of the night, even back then. Things like lighting, the design of the flyers and all the rest was a big part of the experience of the whole night, almost equal to the music.

Not a lot of party promoters pay much attention to the non-musical aspects of the night.

It's so important. Like with the lighting, I try to keep things really simple, with mirror balls, spots and some sharpies, a little bit of fog. For the lighting on the floor we strictly use warm, organic, comfortable colors. We also rarely use any projections, and no strobes either; lasers, sometimes in moderation and class. Also the lighting elsewhere in the club is of equal importance. The entrances need to be dim; hallways, bathrooms — the club should feel like one cohesive, living entity.

Tim Sweeney was one of your first out-of-town guests, right?

Justin and I DJ'ed a gig down in LA, the Black Disco party in LA. Kevin Carney, aka Nitedog, who was throwing them at Mountain Bar in Chinatown, and that was the first time I met Tim Sweeney. We invited him to play FACE later in the year. Besides Tim, we had Jacques Renault, Prince Language, Thomas Bullock.

That list is all New York–based DJs, though Thomas has moved since then. How did you hook up with all those guys?

Since Justin Montag had moved from New York, he was in touch with a lot of those guys and that whole circle. I was too, but initially a bit more remotely; we already kind of all knew of each other in some way. That period of time was very formative for the scene in New York, and in San Francisco as well. It just felt that ideas, tribes, and a shared rhythm was gathering momentum and support. But, really, with FACE, we were kind of doing our own thing.

How so?

Well, San Francisco had a very strong club scene, with stuff like the Wicked parties and all the rest. But I wasn't really part of that scene. I did go to a few of those parties, but I didn't know any of those guys. All we were doing was bringing out our friends, and friends of friends, to play. A lot of the time we would bring people out just because we missed them and wanted to see them, really.

Why go to all that trouble?

It's kind of what I'm used to. I'm used to caring about the whole package, which is something that I think I learned from working at Apple, where we take care of every micron. But also, I've tried to learn as much as possible from working with the likes of Harvey and James Murphy when it comes to this.

Can you give an example?

With Harvey, if you go to a soundcheck with him, for instance, you'll see how he tunes the room, from the needle on outwards. Just seeing how he views the whole night was very influential.

He sees the night as an integrated whole, with all the components fitting together properly.

Yeah, and I've always felt the same way, but just hearing him verbalize it and seeing how he goes about it was a big influence. Because of the obsession with detail, most clubs here find us difficult to work with, but at the same time they appreciate it because they understand we're after something great.

"The entrances need to be dim; hallways, bathrooms — the club should feel like one cohesive, living entity."

You eventually moved the party from Amnesia and made the move out of dive bars, right?

We went to a club called SOM, and then we started doing stuff at Monarch, and Public Works — that was our home for a long time — and then there were some at 1015 Folsom. But more recently, I haven't been doing them under the FACE name. That party was with Justin, along with our other friend Bootsy, who had joined later when we started transitioning out of bars and into proper clubs. Justin is now in LA and Bootsy is now in Oregon, so I thought it was respectful to put the FACE name on pause. The more recent parties are now just a party.

Are there any particular nights, any specific DJ sets, that really stand out? Or is it all a blur by this time?

All the Harvey parties are obviously very special, not just musically, but because his vibe and presence is always exciting. Whenever we have KZA from Force of Nature — he's such an amazing DJ, and always has a great trajectory in his sets — Kenji Takimi, too. The other parties that come to mind are these couple of underground ones that we've done with Jamie xx.

We've done a few undergrounds with Jamie, and typically he's only been quietly announced the night of. People still talk to me about these nights. The warehouse where we've thrown these is sadly no longer there, but it was a massive industrial space, where we set up a smaller club structure within the warehouse, flanked by a mini ramp, and other smaller structures; a pop-up club within the context of a larger party. These nights felt extremely special.

What was the impetus for starting the Public Release label?

Public Release actually began before the label existed, around 2005, as a series of downloadable mixes I made that were on the downtempo vibe, and then started creeping up into housey stuff, but really pretty varied. Those then transitioned into mix CDs, which were in stores like Colette in Paris, and in New York in stores like aNYthing, and here in San Francisco. The name Public Release was supposed to imply that it's a public document, and I'm releasing it for free. It was never meant to turn into an actual record label.

The design aspect has always played a large role in Public Release as well, right?

Yeah, from the start. I got a lot of friends to do the covers for those CDs. A guy named Evan Hecox, who's a legendary illustrator who did a lot for Chocolate Skateboards, did the artwork for the first one. He also designed a little logo for Public Release, made to have the same vibe as the Public Broadcasting Service logo. I was so thankful to Evan that I've kept using the logo to this day.

How did making mix CDs morph into helming a label?

That happened in 2009. The first release was an edits thing with Tim Sweeney with artwork from Shadi Perez, who's a seminal New York photographer. What happened was I went to a gig where Tim was DJ'ing, and he played a track that I loved. I asked him what it was and he went, "Oh, it's this edit I just made." I asked him if anyone else had it and was playing it, he said no, and I said, "Well, we should put it out or something!" He was like, "Let's do it!"

And the end result was Public Release 01, the "Stop Sitting Around/Get Me a Doctor" EP.

Yeah. I had heard him play "Stop Sitting Around," which I think is basically a 45 playing at 33 type of situation. The second release was Jacques Renault edits. Then, the Blackjoy one ["The Jekyll EP," 2011] was the first one that was original music. And then, there was "Mike Simonetti's Circadian Rhythms" EP, which was the last edits release I did under Public Release. As you know, edits are mainly tools for DJs, and I was becoming interested in broadening the scope of what the label could be and where it could go.

In what way?

Not in any kind of ambitious way. It was more that I had a lot of friends who were producing music, and it was difficult for them to easily get it out. I would hear about the politics and all these different issues, and the hurdles they would have to clear just to get this music out. I was like, OK, let's just do it together.

That's a nicely casual ethos.

I've always viewed Public Release almost as an ongoing art project, in the framework of a record label. It's very organic. Things are done over a drink or a text. There's no schedule; when the year starts, there's no set of releases that have to come out. When stuff is ready, it comes out.

I will say that I don't like stuff just sitting around on a hard drive. When it's ready, I do want to get it out to people. At the same time, if something's not quite right, if the artwork's not right, or we need to remaster it for the fourth time, whatever, we'll be patient. There's no rush or financial need.

Most Public Release records seem to just sound really great, audio-wise. Are you hands-on with that end of things?

A while back, I was introduced to George Horn by Josh Cheon at Dark Entries; I've been going to him since Jacques Renault's "Silver Machines" double EP release in 2015. George is this legendary engineer at Fantasy Studios in Berkeley. He's one of the best at his craft, and I enjoy learning from people like that. I started going to George and sitting in on the mastering, and also even the cutting of the lacquer, the making of the physical master which the mold would be made from. That kind of thing really interests me, because that kind of ties in with what I do in industrial design. So yeah, it's a very hands-on approach.

How about other aspects of production?

Musically, whoever the release is from, I try to be a little more hands-off. There's a lot of back-and-forth on the tracklist, but the songs, the structure, the actual track itself, I'll leave that to the artist. The exception is when they ask me for direct feedback, and I'll give it: "This section is too long in my opinion," "This part meanders a little too much," and stuff like that. But most people with releases on the label know exactly what they are doing.

The label is largely American artists, but there are a couple of Brits, Richard Sen and Mark E. How did you meet them?

I still haven't actually met Richard! He's done some remixes for me, and he has one original track on a compilation that we recently released. He's an artist who I actually reached out to. I'm a huge fan of Padded Cell, Bronx Dogs, all that stuff. And I've been a huge fan of Mark's since I was buying his stuff off Jisco. Most recently, Mark and I did the "Shelter" EP release in the summer of 2019, and Richard's first full EP on Public Release will come out in 2021. Prior to these releases, I've done quite a few remixes with them both. Mark and Richard are two of my all-time favorites, and I'm so grateful to be continuing our work together.

Does Public Release have a concrete musical aesthetic, or is it basically just a matter of putting out music that you like, made by people who you like?

I would say the latter. It's really just about releasing music that I enjoy, and I do have a bit of a policy that it's all by friends or at least friends of friends. It's very rare that I'll release something where it starts as a demo sent to me out of the blue. I think that's happened maybe only once. As much as I value the end product, I equally value the process of working on the record together. The process of getting there is something that I find really satisfying.

On the design end of Public Release, you've had quite a few clothing collaborations in recent years. How do those come about?

That's often a friends and friends-of-friends kind of thing, too. For instance, Måns Ericson and I became really great friends since being introduced through Eric Duncan in NY, back when Måns was at Adidas. He had been a fan of the label, and after they got Junior Executive off the ground, he and his partner Nils Schéle asked if we could do something together. We did all the basics that we all loved wearing, but also some silk shirts that came out really nice. I roped in Shadi to shoot the campaign.

Or for the various artists record that Public Release recently put out ["415-PR22" EP], I got Zak David to do the art. Zak is a friend from Vancouver, and he's a legendary graffiti artist called Virus. He's been working at Supreme for over a decade. The mushroom man he created for the release … I think everyone can relate to the expression on his face right now. Anyway, I was texting Måns some images of the mushroom man — Måns is doing some work with Très Bien, which is a big [menswear] label out of Sweden — and he was like, "Why don't we do something?" And now I have a small collection coming out on Très Bien, centered around this mushroom guy.

We also have a little edits label called It's a Feeling with a friend who will go unnamed for now. The graphic on those releases was by Fergus [Purcell], who does a lot of design work for Palace — we love very much how the Feeling part of that looks. Fergus also does stuff for IDEA Books in London, which is run by my buddies Angela and David, and we ended up using that Feeling graphic for sort of a triple partnership with them and Nonnative. I actually had the opportunity to design a DJ bag with Nonnative a few years ago, because I had been frustrated with the bags that were available. All these things happen because of all these connections.

You seem to have a lot of those connections!

We've actually collaborated with quite a few notable artists in various ways, and I have an ongoing relationship with most of them. They're typically close friends. Shadi, Virus, Fergus, Yoko Takahashi, Sk8thing, Takeshi Murata, Hassan Rahim, Barry McGee … Barry is definitely one of the artists most closely connected with the label. He's done quite a bit of work with us, not only album covers, but tour graphics, posters, graphics for clothing, all types of ephemera. It's a real honor to have Barry in the mix, and the process is always a bit unexpected and unique. He's probably the only artist or designer that I work with that hands in actual original artwork. No scans, nothing digital. He'll give me a stack of options all hand painted, often littered with Letraset type experiments, stuffed into a folder, that's then wrapped in a brown paper bag. It's sometimes given to me directly, but often times just left on my doorstep late at night. I love it, it's so immediate, so analog, lo-fi and not a big deal.

Producing music can be thought of as a kind of design, yet you aren't a producer. Why is that?

I get asked that a lot! Even by friends. "Why aren't you making your own beats?" I just haven't felt the urge. I think there's already so much great music out that I haven't felt the need to make my own music. That might come in part from my background as a DJ.

How's that?

I'm quite used to, and content with, playing other people's music to create a story that's my own.

"Things are done over a drink or a text. There's no schedule."

Which is also a form of design, in a way.

Totally. And there's that unique form of a song that pops up for a very short period when you are mixing two records together, and it's its own thing for just that moment in time. I find that really fun.

It's interesting that as a DJ and a guy who runs a vinyl-oriented label, your day job is working for a company that, in a lot of ways, has transformed the way in which we think about music, or at least how we consume music. It's become something ethereal and abstract.

I do find the convenience of music pretty interesting, and while it's obviously great that we can access all this music any time we want, there is a lot that gets lost. I was just speaking with a friend about how much we miss record liner notes, for instance. Even just the thank yous; you could learn so much about the artist, and the people behind them, through all those little clues and hidden references. There'd be a trail of breadcrumbs that you could follow. You can't get that through an MP3 or a stream. **R**

Vanessa Worm

Tessa Forde, otherwise known as Vanessa Worm, has emerged as an artistic force in a relatively short period, thanks in part to her releases on Glasgow's Optimo Music. Taking everything that's swirling around within her, Forde converts it all into her music and spontaneous live performances. Having grown up near the southern tip of New Zealand, Forde spent some formative years in Melbourne, where the absence of the music she wanted to hear put her on her artistic path. Now she's back, and embracing the New Zealand scene with open arms.

Interview – Karl Henkell
Photography – Ruby Harris

Growing up where you did, the land you were surrounded by gave you quite a bit of freedom. From the sound of it you could make as much noise as you wanted?

Yes. So I grew up in Winton, on like a 20 acre livestock block, or whatever you can call it. My dad's a sheep shearer, and he's actually got world records in sheep shearing. So he's always told me that, and this has stuck with me forever. It's like the most ingrained, awesomest thing stuck in my head is that if you put your mind to it, you can do anything. So I was really blessed to have that phrase given to me so young. So that was with me, from really young. And yeah, my parents were quite busy, but they were really loving and just kind of let us basically do whatever we wanted. And I really enjoyed "Hannah Montana," and Disney was a huge part of my desire to perform music and sing, and like my first guitar was a "Hannah Montana" guitar, but I think that's probably where I was able to realize that I liked music. So it wasn't like, people around me were doing music or you know, there wasn't much, so I would put it down to Hannah Montana I'd say and yeah just having freedom to do whatever.

If you wanted to sing in a field, no one was gonna stop you or judge you or anything.

Yeah, I used to sing mostly, we had quite a huge lawn. So we'd have this wee motorbike and we'd tie a rope and like a sack to the back of it. We would sit on the sack and my sister would drive the motorbike around and do like skids and stuff. And then that's when I would sing most of the time, [*laughs*] because I was just having so much fun, and you're just singing so loud and you're just like, "Fuck yeah." That was so much fun. That was pretty wild. Yeah, but actually with singing, when I was in year five or something, so must have been like 10, I told myself I would never, ever sing in front of people again, and then this big fear of singing built up in me. So that's been a huge, huge thing. Because it's not just singing, it's like fear of being, just being, like fear of just allowing yourself to express freely without any resistance. But everybody has that on some level.

Was there something in particular that happened? Like someone, I don't know, telling you off while singing or something?

I don't know. I have no idea. My first primary school was like, super awesome, and I had an awesome principal and he'd play guitar and sing with us. I remember him singing, I remember that interaction, that's when I first realized like, "I really want to know more about singing, I really like it." But then I went to a different primary school after that, which was in

year five, which is when I started singing, which would have been when I was 10, and it was an all girls primary school, and it was quite like, not — I'm a bit rough around the edges and like, not real girly and shit. And they were quite strict and like you all had to line up in your houses and take a step forward and go, "Good morning Mrs. McKay." It wasn't like the nicest environment for me, personally, and I don't know, maybe it was just this like rebellion to the system. Like I'm not going to participate in school singing or, I don't know, it's probably the most logical thing I could put it to, but otherwise I got no idea. There's probably fears as well. It was probably the age where I started to get self-conscious, like puberty and stuff. That makes more sense. Just natural like, pubescent insecurities.

Did you play in bands in high school?

Yes. Also boarding school, same sort of thing where just like, boarding school wasn't for me. Like, just living around catty girls not for me either, but there was one girl at boarding school called Mackenzie, and her and I just got on so good, and she was a drummer. And I was playing guitar at the time. And we lived together at this boarding school and just would spend all of our time doing music together. And then we started a band together and, yeah we would play just like school band and stuff. And we would just share our passion for music with each other. Also boarding school is when I started making electronic music as well, because you could hide yourself in your bed and just like, put your headphones on and put everything away and just play on Logic. We had laptops at school as well, so I spent 9 till 3 p.m. pretty much just watching live bands on YouTube, just doing everything to get away from the school and just be immersed in this world of music online, which is not actually any music I'm into now. My taste and everything's completely changed. But, at the time, it was pretty fun. It's actually probably the most passionate, I think, I've ever felt about music.

So that was kind of the start of you playing around with music on computers?

Yeah, because I started recording guitar and stuff on Logic, and then I just started playing around with their built-in instruments and stuff. And it was fricken' whack. Like the stuff I was making was just—

You wouldn't show anyone now?

I wouldn't release it, but like I would show people like, "Listen to this fucked up shit." Because it's unlike anything. And it's not like it's necessarily bad, it's just such a sound you just don't hear it anywhere. But I've lost all that stuff now. [*laughs*]

"I just want to be like in this crowd of people, like on a microphone, directing the space so fucking badly. That's just all I wanted to do when I'd go out."

Your interest in what lay outside of New Zealand, you already had that when you were in your teens? Like wanting to move to Melbourne you said came up pretty early?

Yeah, really young. Even younger than that. Not even necessarily Melbourne, but just to go to like, a city. I really wanted to go to New York for just, I can't remember at what age it was when I started thinking about these things, but just fricken', my whole heart and soul was in the idea that I'll be in New York one day. And I think that a lot of that just came from like, the media that I was consuming, a lot was just your typical sort of movies or Disney Channel and stuff, and there's this whole like fascination about big city living. So I think that just did it.

When I first went to Melbourne, I was only there for three months. But when I went back over again, and moved over permanently — well, for three years, or whatever, two years — I was going out to clubs there and I, by this time, I was sort of making music, and I just felt there was something really lacking. When I would go there, there was just a certain vibe and a certain energy that I personally wanted to experience and I wasn't getting it.

So that's why I made "[I Did A] Lava Dance" and did that first EP and I was, "This is what I wanna hear." Not that there wasn't oomph, but to me, what feels oomph-y, which takes a fucking lot, to be honest. And I also just visualized and just saw myself as like I just want to be like in this crowd of people, like on a microphone, directing the space so fucking badly. That's just all I wanted to do when I'd go out. That was my intention behind the first EP, so that's how Melbourne kind of shaped me there.

Was performing always part of it for you, the intention to produce stuff that you could then perform rather than producing to DJ, like many people do?

Definitely, because as soon as I realized that I wanted to be a singer, that's when I started Vanessa Worm and like, the vocals used to be really scream-y, and then I got to Melbourne, and it was more commanding and things like Meredith [Music Festival], real, real scream-y.

And [Animals Dancing], that was much more immersive, it was a nice togetherness. The singing thing was why I did Vanessa Worm originally, not knowing it would lead to that. And then I didn't wanna DJ, because I didn't really listen to any music, and like why should I DJ when I'm not collecting music and when I'm not like a music enthusiast and all of that? You know, I'd rather someone who's passionate about it and has something to offer in that regards do that. So I wasn't gonna pretend. Even though I have DJ'ed and I do really, really enjoy doing it. But there's a time and a place for me to do that, performance was definitely the main thing.

Does it come from a love of live music and punk music, that live aspect of crowd-surfing and, you know, engaging with the crowd in that way? It's not very "DJ at a nightclub in the corner."

Definitely, from watching live performances and being a fan of "Hannah Montana" and just always wanting to perform. And then going to Melbourne, I wasn't feeling like I was connecting with people on the level that I would like to, so I thought well, I felt that was something I could offer by performing. I could maybe offer that connection to people, offer the opportunity to feel that connection with each other, on that really personal level, where you've got someone in the crowd with you, fucking like, dancing and like doing the energy shit. I feel like I have so much to say as well. And I feel like, and I've got so much like, burdened energy as well, and that comes out heaps in performance. And it's just an opportunity for me to let out some shit. And it's an opportunity for other people to let out some shit if they want to.

Did it take a lot for you to get up for the first time to perform? Is it something you have to psych yourself up for?

Yes and no. It's something I have heaps of trust in. Like, I've got so much trust in the performance. Like, no matter what goes down. I just know I'll be OK. I don't know where that's come from. I'm like that with life as well. Just in general I'm just like, "Well, whatever the fuck happens, like, I'm gonna be fine." Like, I'm still human, still a person. That holds me through performances.

"I feel like, and I've got so much like,
burdened energy as well, and that comes out
heaps in performance."

"It's like a snake, you've gotta shed the skin to do something new."

Also noticed [that] when I had lots of gigs and if there was one I was really nervous for, I would create stories in my mind to kind of balance out the insecurity or the nervousness or the doubts, and then create stories in my mind that opposed those. And that enabled me to get up and play Meredith, for example, or do these really big things that I had never done before.
But then you kind of get hit with the reality. Like so many months later, where you're like, "Well, that, what I made myself believe to get up there isn't actually true."
And then those doubts will resurface and then you sit with them however many months later. So that's one way I think like psyching myself up for a performance has happened in the past.

A lot of the times I can't talk before a show at all, because I'm just feeling so, so, so much. I just can't speak with people at all. And if I do, what I mean to say isn't coming out and it can be really intense, because you're dealing with [being] about to perform.
But then you're also dealing with like, "Oh my God, I hope these people don't, you know, view me as being rude because I can't speak properly." So you're dealing with everything in your mind and then your body all at once. [laughs] But that also comes down to if you've had a really good sleep and prepared yourself in that way and you've spent the day like, being centered, that's a bit different and that's probably something that I should lean into more.

You've mentioned not making music all the time, only when you feel like it. Is that something you still do?

Yeah, 100%. That's huge for me. Same with making the album. That was very much so with that, I could not force a single thing. I sat there and tried to force something, it would be a flop and I'd end up in a shitty [mood], because it wasn't working. So it hugely comes down to inspiration, and a lot of the music I would make like within the hour so it'd be, get the inspiration, sit at the computer and then out would pop a song, and there were times where you'd go to make music and I wouldn't get any further than just like a bassline, and then just have to scratch it and then it was very rare that, like a whole song would be made.

And then now, similar sort of thing, but my instinct is telling me to start being a bit more scheduled and start doing it more. So it's still coming from that place of inspiration. So it's not like I'm sitting here and going,

"Right, I need to do this every single day." Maybe I am, or I have to ask myself that but I've gotta do it this time and this time. And like, there is no part of it that is forced. I just think that me forcing something, just doesn't work. [laughs]

You mentioned having to move on from music you made to make something new. Do you feel that way about your album "Vanessa 77" even though you have love for it, that you have to put it behind you to create something new?

I feel like that's already kind of been put behind me, to a tee. So there's this whole story of "Vanessa 77," a whole persona, a whole like version of myself that was "Vanessa 77" that, like, you know, if I didn't have those beliefs, that lyrical content would have been different. And it all just, it all plays the same role, and then I don't know when it was, but this year, like so many of those beliefs, have just been, like, ripped away. Like, as not truth anymore. Just that whole person I was has completely just gone, pretty much, on some level. And I think that's just a process of like, death and rebirth, I guess. And that's kind of what the album was about as well. It was about death and rebirth, on some level, that I wasn't so consciously aware of. I'm not too sure, but I reckon that's just gonna continue to happen with every sort of musical endeavour though, and every sort of project and idea and every phase of your life. It's like a snake, you've gotta shed the skin to do something new.

And then it's a cycle that keeps on going, because you put so much into a project that it's only normal that you'd maybe just have to feel some relief and shed it off, to move on.

Yeah. And also because the way I create music, is very much so, from my experience, you know, it's really expressive. Because I don't plan, like, I'm not going, "I'm gonna make this sort of sound," or with "Vanessa 77" anyway there was no room for me to go, "I'm gonna make this sound and then do these lyrics." There was no sort of structure to it. It was just, "This is who I am." And it was just done in a moment.

And that's why for me there's such a huge experience of transformation between projects. Because I put my whole soul on the table. And I'm sure everyone does, maybe.

"I feel fucking everything so, yeah. And I think it's important.
Like I live by feeling the shit things as well."

You talked about having to face your fears in the writing of the album. Does that voice come out in the album at all? I don't know if I'm reading into it too much but you kind of manipulated your voice to sound quite warped, and it can feel a bit uncomfortable at times. Kind of like the voices in your head that swirl around?

Yeah. I'd have to sit with that thought, and have a listen, since I haven't thought about it like that.

I might be reading too much into it? [*laughs*]

There's definitely something there with what you're saying ... There was a lot at the time that I was kind of just — there were a lot of questions I had, a lot of anger as well, that I had. And yeah, just heaps of feelings. I feel things, like I'm really sensitive in that sense. And I feel fucking everything so, yeah. And I think it's important. Like I live by feeling the shit things as well.

And sometimes those shit feelings, like I was saying, a thought might get put on to that feeling that isn't ... probably a lot of what's on the album is a pure expression of a lot of that shit. Like just crap and just like putting that into, just, it's just a way to give that feeling a voice. Because I think sometimes we don't give everything a voice.

It's almost by giving it a voice that maybe you can move on from it too?

Fucking 100%. And learn from it as well. Like sometimes I sit here a year later after having made the song. Especially earlier this year and I'd listened to the song every time, it was just like I was learning something new about what I was saying. Like I realized more and more and more each time I was like, "Oh my God, this is gonna be never-ending."

I mean, it seems like this whole few years for you has been a huge journey of growth. Do you feel like there's more growing to be done?

Heaps! [*chuckles*] Yeah, God, yeah. I'm only 22, but that whole period of time, 18 to 21, 22 feels very, like, just getting your feet, and then now I feel like I've got my feet, kind of, somewhat.

Like I saw a wee ant on a tree the other day. And what that showed me was that I am like that ant on that tree and that tree is that world of like, knowledge and wisdom. And to that ant that tree goes forever, and that's the same with life, for every single person on this planet, like, there's always more to learn.

And I think that's an important thing to realize that, you know, you don't know everything. Things might shock you, and you might get everything that you believe questioned. And I think that's a really good attitude to be in as well, while we kind of set up, you know, new ways of doing things in the future because things are changing. I don't know how we're meant to solve, for example, like an economic crisis if we think we know everything. If we can sit there and listen to each other and be the student at the same time as we're all teaching each other, you know? I think that is a way forward. That is really important that people start recognizing.

With things opening back up in New Zealand, how was the experience of going to a festival and being amongst people again?

It was really intense to begin with. We arrived at this house where we were staying with like 15 people. It took a few days to settle in and get used to social interaction again. It was really nice because everyone there … this was with [Club] 121, every one of them is just super loving and welcoming to all sorts of people. They're all about you can be and do whatever you want as long as you're kind to one another. And the gigs as well, I found that … they were really great because 121 were bringing these gigs to Raglan or especially Tauranga, where they've never really had any house music or techno gigs there, and bringing it there and showing it to these people who have never heard it before, and experiencing that. And seeing people who have never danced to house music get into it. It's sick. Obviously no international people are here at the moment either so it's just all about, so many Kiwis are getting onboard.

Since New Zealand is basically COVID-free, you can have gigs.

Well New Zealand has basically kept COVID out. There is no COVID in New Zealand. Everything is fully back to normal, festivals are just as they would be, gigs just as they would be, bars are open. That's what's been really good for New Zealand, because it's just been all of these locals getting together and really showcasing what New Zealand has. And I really feel like … there is just so much goodness here, and so much, in my experience anyway, a lot of love and support between musicians and artists, and I think New Zealand is quite young in what it has yet to show, and it's really good that everyone is getting the opportunity to work together and create new things, and I think New Zealand may blossom a lot, in the next few years, especially musically. I like to think so, anyway. **R**

"It's just been all of these locals getting together and really showcasing what New Zealand has. And I really feel like … there is just so much goodness here."

Ana Roxanne

From the entry point of classic R&B singers, Ana Roxanne's path through choral singing, a formative experience in India, and a stint at an experimental music college have led her to develop as an artist comfortable with using her voice as her primary instrument.

Gentle and enveloping, Roxanne's songs give listeners the feeling of eavesdropping on a private catharsis in progress. Los Angeles-raised and now based in New York, her music practice offers her solace and fosters an evolving relationship with herself and the world.

Interview – Glen Goetze
Photography – Tanya and Zhenya Posternak

"I remember being extremely mesmerized by her and her style, and just kind of deciding right then and there that I wanted to be a singer"

Is music a full-time affair for you these days?

It is, kind of. My goal is to make it more so in terms of money, but I guess it's full-time. I feel like I'm always thinking about it or always doing something related to it. Even if I'm working a random food service job.

Did you grow up in a particularly musical family?

No one was formally trained, but my parents definitely listened to a lot of music. My dad really liked classical music and oldies and stuff, and my mom was very into R&B, disco and I guess pop, but my parents both sing for fun too. My mom and her sisters sang a lot in church. That's kind of where I got a lot of my musical beginnings, from being around or hearing the music they would play and hearing my mom and her sisters singing, and by going to church and hearing it there.

Do you remember the first time a particular piece of music resonated with you?

I remember when I was really young, I was really into Mariah Carey and I would always watch or listen whenever it came on the radio or whatever. We had the tape that I would always listen to. I guess in my early years that's sort of what comes to mind, and also Toni Braxton's first album, that was played a lot in my household.

Then in middle school when I started to think about being a singer myself and I was sort of playing with that idea and feeling inspired, it was kind of from Alicia Keys' first single, "Fallin'." I remember being extremely mesmerized by her and her style, and just kind of deciding right then and there that I wanted to be a singer and I wanted to take it seriously, and I wanted to find out how to sing like her, how to be like her. So that was a pinnacle moment for me.

I would travel with my jazz crew sometimes, and we would do competitions. It just became a very big thing for me, and that's kind of all I wanted to do, I didn't really care about school that much.

What are your listening habits like?

Sometimes I feel like I get really stuck, I get obsessed with vocalists, and I feel like that's when I listen to music the most. I love pop, I'm obsessed with pop and I'm obsessed with R&B divas, and I get really fixated or I have like a rotation, I guess, of divas that I'm constantly listening to, it's almost like a vocal practice for me. I'm sort of spending time singing along and just practicing my own vocal cords, my instruments, my muscles, it's like scales on a piano.

If you're doing your vocal exercises, what are you listening to?

It's sort of embarrassing, but I am deeply obsessed with Ariana Grande. I also love classic divas of the 20th century, like Mariah, Whitney, Toni Braxton. I'm always cycling through them, like Nina Simone, Aretha Franklin. A lot of these are hard to sing along to, it's more like a deep listening exercise, but still feeling very touched and moved by it. I'm always trying to find new pop music that I feel connected to, but it's sort of rare for me to find a new artist where I vibe with both their vocal technique and their music, the songwriting and production.

I read that a trip to India was a formative experience for you. Did this impact your perspective or where you were heading at the time?

I was north of New Delhi. It was another one of those random decisions, kind of on a whim. A friend of mine was living there and I just wanted to visit. I was supposed to be there for just a few weeks on vacation. Once I was there, it was a really intense experience, I met this music teacher and I was studying yoga too, and it just felt really important to continue those studies. I had just quit a job working with kids that I was super burnt out on. I was about to go back to school for music, at Mills to study electronic music. I was about to start a new job working at a different school. I ended up deferring the semester, and then I quit my job over the phone, then I stayed for a couple more months. I was there for a total of three months. It was one of those mid-20s spiral moments. My parents were really mad at me, no one really understood what I was doing. I didn't even really know what I was doing, but it ended up working out for the best.

That served as the catalyst, being introduced to that tradition of music just really blew my mind, and it opened up these other possibilities of performance and composition.

> "I have like a rotation, I guess, of divas that I'm constantly listening to, it's almost like a vocal practice for me."

Had you had any experience playing or performing music at that point in time?

I did kind of, informally. I never took music lessons or voice lessons growing up. I did theater as a kid, so sometimes it would be musicals and then that was sort of an intro to performing or singing, but I never had any formal training. Anything that I was doing, it was kind of just like by copying what I heard.

I never took piano as a kid, my parents never forced that on me, but I did get very serious about choir when I was in high school. Even then I wasn't taking any theory classes or playing any instruments, but I was just constantly singing in a jazz group or in a choral ensemble.

When you say you got serious, you really enjoyed it or you really wanted to be good at it?

I guess both. I really enjoyed it. I played some sports, but I was definitely always more interested in music.

"Discovering the practice, or this tradition, it can be very self-contained. I could just have this very beautiful full musical experience with basically just me singing"

I had always been interested in classical Indian music, but I didn't really know that much about it, and when I met [the music teacher] I had heard her perform this song, and for the first time it sort of just blew my mind, and I felt like I needed to learn about that tradition and study with her. It was very stripped down, there was a drone element, there was a rhythmic element, a tabla, and then it was just her singing. There was no amplification, just sitting on the floor in a room together, and I was so moved by this simple little demo performance. At that time I still hadn't been writing any music, my own experiences being in jazz bands was singing music that other people had written.

If I hadn't done that I don't think I would've written any of this music. I took that and then started at Mills finally and then I was learning about electronic music and avant-garde composers, and then that's when I finally started writing music of my own. So all these influences that came together — the jazz training in my early college years and that program that I dropped out of in the Midwest, and then India — it all just came together.

How do you think it factors into how you make music?

When I heard her sing, the whole setup was so simple and it was just about her voice. And I was noticing when I was traveling there, just seeing how much music was tied into daily life and also tied in with religion and spirituality.

Being in jazz school and then also playing in these bands where I wasn't writing anything, or I was kind of new at playing an instrument; singing was always my main instrument, but it never felt like enough, because I had to rely on someone to accompany me. Just discovering the practice, or this tradition, it can be very self-contained. I could just have this very beautiful full musical experience with basically just me singing, and then having a very minimal accompaniment. Seeing that setup be so mind-blowing and powerful in its simplicity, but also it's not simple, it's so deep and, I don't know, it was just really cool! It just opened my eyes to the possibilities of being just a singer and not seeing that as a weakness. It changed how I viewed my strength and my ability to construct something.

What led you to Mills College? Was it somewhat renowned as an art school?

Yeah, I didn't even really know that much about it, I would just hear about it, because I spent some years in the Midwest going to school and then eventually dropping out, and just working and playing in a couple of bands and hanging out. I finally moved back to the Bay Area and I was just working, and I was thinking about how I never really thought about the idea of being an artist, trying to make that my main focus in life. It always felt like, "Oh, it can only be like a hobby, or it can only be this side passion that I have."

"I had never written any original music of my own. I always had ideas, but I never knew how to express them."

girls who were fresh out of high school and then also women who are close to my mother's age, and we were all making these 30-second noise compositions on vintage synths together, it was really crazy. It was really interesting and formative for me.

Are there any particular lessons you learned there that stuck with you?

One of my main mentors there was this woman, Maggi Payne, she really helped me to come into my own as a composer. I had gone into that school not really having any experience, I had never written any original music of my own. I always had ideas, but I never knew how to express them. I remember feeling so intimidated, I would write some assignment or a 30-second thing for homework, and not be able to tell, "Is it good enough?" I always felt like my writing was too simple or boring, and she was very reassuring to me and encouraging. I remember eventually she told me that she saw me as a composer. It was so simple, but for her to actually just say that to me, I feel like no one had really said that to me before, and it gave me this boost of confidence and self-assuredness of like, "Oh, maybe I do know what I'm doing and maybe I should trust that I can make music. It doesn't matter if I'm new to it, it doesn't matter if I've played in bands or I wasn't really writing songs." It didn't matter, as long as I was doing it, and enjoyed doing it, and felt like I had something that I wanted to express. So that really stuck with me, having that validation from Mills, especially a femme-identified person telling me that, and she is a really amazing composer too. I definitely take that with me wherever I go.

How did you start focusing on making songs and making something more fully realized for yourself?

I guess a lot of the ideas for a lot of those songs [on "~~~"] I'd actually written during my time at Mills. It all sort of came together when I started learning about different avant-garde composers, learning about Erik Satie and the history of ambient music. I didn't really know anything about ambient music and so I think learning about these different composers helped me to see what had been done and what the intention was behind it. I felt very drawn towards that and so that's when it all sort of started coming together for me, that's when I was gathering all of these different influences that I had growing up that were very important to me and very deeply a part of my personal music practice, but that had no way of being expressed really, outside of karaoke or being in jazz school.

But I was just working a ton and feeling kind of burnt out, and so I was sort of just toying with the idea of going back to finish my music degree, and I would just hear about Mills and how it was like this experimental music thing, where they had the music program that was not super traditional, but I didn't really know that much about its history. I took a tour and I just had this feeling that I wanted to be there.

I honestly didn't have that much experience going into it, so it was interesting to seriously jump in and start from scratch. In my first few years of college in the Midwest I was in a jazz program, studying jazz and classical music, so by the time I got to Mills I had some musical training under my belt, but it was more in a traditional sense, so it was nice to be able to have that and then also be in this experimental program and be able to combine those two schools of thought.

How was your experience there?

It was amazing, it was also the first time that I was exposed to or had a formal education in feminism or intersectional feminism and how that could relate to art and music, and learning about women in music was a huge eye-opener for me, thinking about music and gender for the first time. Also historically Mills has been an all women's college. I think in later years they've allowed men to be a part of the graduate programs. So I did go to school with some men, but most of my classes were just women, ranging from age 18 to middle age, and I remember taking an electronic music class, and it was so cool to be with really young

"A lot of my songs come about if I'm processing an emotion or an experience, but it becomes this space where I can sort of sink into it and feel kind of at peace."

I'm curious about how you arrived on that more ambient sound, is it something you were just into, or you felt it suited your voice, or was it something you weren't hearing?

I think I just really loved drone. When I was studying with my teacher in India, I would be doing these vocal exercises to a drone, and just thinking about that structure, it just became like a meditative practice for me and I would just get lost in it. Then my friend let me play with his delay pedal and that was my first time playing with a delay pedal, and that's when I started composing stuff and I was like, "Oh wow, yeah, drone." [*laughs*]

How does a piece of music come about for you, do you have a particular process or starting point?

It's a little random, I think. I like the idea of creating music that creates a calming atmosphere. A lot of my songs come about if I'm processing an emotion or an experience, but it becomes this space where I can sort of sink into it and feel kind of at peace. Even if I'm feeling upset or sad or confused, it's just like this sort of safe, cozy space to me. But I think of it more as creating an environment of sorts, creating a mood. I find that lyrical content always comes last. I think of a mood and then I sort of feel a melody, and then words come later. I know a lot of songwriters who think about the lyrics first or something, but that's just how it's been for me and it might change because I still feel like I'm very new, and I'm still figuring it out.

How did "Because of a Flower" all coalesce conceptually, what was the glue that made it make sense to you?

That EP ["~~~"] came out, and with everything after that, I noticed I was writing stuff that was very influenced by my confusion or feelings about gender identity. And so I just noticed that that could be a concept. I didn't even really think of it like that at first, I would just write songs, and naturally that's just what I wanted to write about over those years. And then when I became public about my identity, that was around the time that I had signed the deal with Leaving [Records], so at that point, it started to become this little idea in my mind, like, "OK, this EP is getting released." I have these songs and I've just become public about my identity. It might be nice, or it could be healing to me to just dedicate the entire album to it. I just felt a need to put it all together and then maybe just be done with it, you know?

Is the theme explicit? If somebody didn't know anything about you and just picked up the record, would they understand where you're coming from? Or is it a little bit more personal?

I think it's kind of vague in a lot of ways. I wanted it to not be super in-your-face, to be able to have people just experience the music without having to be bombarded. It was more important for me to capture the moods or the feelings rather than being super explicit, with words and lyrics.

I like the idea of having both kinds of experiences or some people not knowing anything about that part of my life. Maybe still being able to get something out of just hearing the music. But then I've spent a lot of time thinking about the concepts and the historical references and cultural references, and I would hope if people are interested they can look deeper into it and find the details or understand the thought behind it.

"I'll be working on a song and basically thinking it's terrible for so long. And then enough time passes and I go, 'Oh, actually, wait, I really like this,' and then it's my favorite thing."

What would you say you learnt about yourself through the process of making the record?

I'm just realizing how important it is to me. Like how much I needed to do it. I had a lot of conflict about it, like, "Oh, should I do this?" Or like, "Is this weird?" Having all these, like, very critical thoughts, and just feeling really unsure about it for a while, because it's also super vulnerable. But I guess I've realized how important it is, and it feels really good actually to finish it. I feel proud of it, even though it's super scary, but I'm really excited to share it.

When you're making music, are you always thinking about it being released, is that on your mind? Or is there a thought that maybe it will just be for you?

I don't know if I really think about the potential of it to be released. I just have to like it and it takes a long time for me to decide if I like something. [*laughs*] I'll be working on a song and basically thinking it's terrible for so long. And then enough time passes and I go, "Oh, actually, wait, I really like this," and then it's my favorite thing. [*laughs*]

I feel like that's a part of a lot of people's process, varying degrees of loathing, loving and back again.

Yeah, it's so heavy. [*laughs*] I want to get over that and quiet the hypercritical voice, allowing myself to just be a little bit more free and just experiment with more things, rather than writing one song a year. [*laughs*]

Were you sharing music with anybody throughout the process of writing "Because of a Flower" for encouragement or feedback?

Very rarely. A couple of close friends, but I would share it live. I'm always more interested in the performance aspect and the intimacy of the live setting, rather than recording or showing somebody a recording or the process of recording. I can't — not that I hate it, but it's really intense. I was going crazy trying to finish this album and I would share it live and that was my way of experimenting with it, seeing how people reacted. But I'm still very private and during the writing process it's very solitary. I also super rarely collaborate just because it's been really intense for me to write music.

Given that the nature of the music is so personal, how do you feel about standing in front of people and sharing it like that?

It's this weird thing where I'm a pretty shy or reserved person, in some ways. In a weird way, it's like I feel more comfortable when I'm singing or performing, because that is something that I've worked on and have control over and it's very intentional and rehearsed and meaningful to me. It is very personal and intimate, and it's exhausting sometimes, to kind of "go there." [*laughs*] But I really like doing it. Especially because the intimacy and the vulnerability, those two concepts are central to the music that I have been writing. So creating an atmosphere like that is really cool to me. Rather than making a record and just putting it out and not performing. It's really important to have that physical space.

That's just how it has been for me. Performing kind of comes naturally, probably because I performed a lot when I was younger. I was homeschooled for most of my childhood, but I did this after school program, so that was my entire social life, my entire world. So I wasn't developing normally in the social sense because I was isolated. But then when it came to performing like that, that was my biggest asset or skill, and I think I carried that through to my adulthood. For better or worse, I don't know. [*laughs*]

Do you think there's something in the music communicating who you are without necessarily having to have conversations?

A lot of the time I'm bad at small talk. Going back to the concept of the album, most of the songs I wrote before I was even out publicly, and so it was a way for me to express this part of myself. No one knew what I was referring to, and it was very vague, but it was more for me to be able to have that space and know that, eventually, I wanted to be public. I wanted to be more expressive about it but that was all I had at the time. It was important to be able to have that mode of expression without being explicit or without talking about it, in conversation. It's been a journey. [*laughs*] **R**

Oskar Mann

Oskar Mann is evidence that a life in and around music can take many forms. After moving to New York from Australia at a young age, he studied jazz through high school and university. Not long after, Mann landed a stint assisting Mark Ronson in the studio, and spent years on the airwaves, broadcasting on East Village Radio. Today, Mann runs Book Works, a music-infused clothing label known for making fun and unexpected objects, that circle concepts of practice and the canon of popular music and jazz standards, the Great American Songbook.

Interview – Karl Henkell
Photography – Kyle Knodell

"Anything pre-internet feels bigger to me, you know, in that how you got to that decision was a very different way to how we make decisions now"

What are some of your earliest musical memories? Growing up, was there music on at home? Were you all playing instruments from a young age?

My grandparents, who I never met, started this record store in Melbourne, which then became the family business, and my first job after school in primary school was essentially stocktaking, you know, and I would get paid a record a week, which was complete child abuse but, you know. I guess when the family's hiring you, I couldn't file a complaint to anyone or anything.

Just being in the shop, but it wasn't necessarily something that we had at home. My dad had a different relationship to music. We never had music on as background [music], it was more very intentional listening.

Was your dad running the record shop for a while or who were you working for?

My dad was involved. I think he was more involved very early on. He was involved with the shop and there were several labels that were offshoots to do with the shop. And my grandparents did a lot of recording and my dad was involved on the recording side with that. It was my uncle who was running the shop at the time.

What was the shop called?

In its first iteration, it was Discurio.

Which became the Book Works T-shirt graphic?

Yes, which gave birth to the angel.

The stuff that they were releasing, was that a particular genre, how would you describe it?

The stuff that I've revisited was really early Aboriginal recordings and indigenous Australian recordings. They were also famously known for the first Barry Humphries record and kind of spoken word stuff. I never think of having a connection with [Dame] Edna Everage, but I guess I do. [*laughs*]

Was that a normal thing for a record store to be doing, to have a record label offshoot?

They also had a radio show too. My grandfather had a radio program, I think it was like the natural progression, you know from record shop to imprint, to distributor, to, you know, take your pick.

Were your parents and extended family an influence on you musically?

Yeah. So, both my parents were in the arts, or artists. My mum is a painter. My dad was a writer/composer of sorts, you know, and that was really, their friend group, our circles were artists. And so that's what I grew up with, that was normal, you know. It was normal and that way of thinking was encouraged.

This is up until like the age of 10 that you're in Melbourne?

When I was 10, I think I was in grade 4, my dad went on this extensive European tour, which I tagged along for. Everyone in my entire primary school was excited that I was leaving for months, like it hadn't happened before. "He's out!"

Was he performing?

Yeah, his band was performing. And I was kind of the roadie slash, you know, tagalong. That tour wound up having this North American leg, and we wound up in New York. And then my dad wanted to move here, so I came along.

And was that a big move back then to get up and move to New York?

To me, it felt big, but at the same time, it felt normal in that it was all I knew, it was all that happened. Yeah, it was big. Anything pre-internet feels bigger to me, you know, in that how you got to that decision was a very different way to how we make decisions now, you know.

That's true. And so, just to place it a bit, what year was it?

We first came in '94. I started school here in '96.

Did you go to a school that was arts-based, music-based?

I wound up going to LaGuardia, which is the "Fame" school. And I always say "Fame," because of the film. I started at Eastside Community High and I was there for middle school. And then to do with the difference in the Australian school system and the American school system where I was at, they thought, "Oh you can just go straight to high school." Even though I was a couple of years younger than everyone else.

And having just moved here, and not knowing anything about the New York public education system. It's such a universe within itself, the schools here. Somehow my dad found out about LaGuardia and managed to get me an audition, because you have to audition to go there. He arranged an audition the day before classes started in September and this is in '97. And I went there and I auditioned on saxophone, which I'd been studying for a while, and was accepted, and then was kind of thrown in the deep end, which was such a shock after what I'd known in Melbourne, you know.

Is it quite demanding, the school?

It was just like, I think in my charming little primary school, there was something like 120 kids, you know. To then go to a high school which was an entire city block with 2,500 kids, you know.

Wow, yeah, that's a lot.

It was just a huge shift, and the way that the days were structured there, where you spent half the day in your studio, whether that was music, art, dance, drama, and then half the day was academics, like regular classes.

But the great thing, in my experience at least, the academic teachers knew that the kids really weren't there for, you know, traditional classes. So, it was very lenient and if you showed that you were taking your studio seriously, they encouraged it. It was really special.

Is that where your love of jazz came from?

Strangely [it was] before that. I was really drawn to bebop, and my dad got me a saxophone when I was 6. So I started playing when I was quite young, and taking lessons, and then piano, and the jazz, specifically bebop, I just really gravitated towards. So then in high school, we were playing, you know, more traditional big band stuff, but everything, you know, and it just opened the floodgates.

Was the move to New York culturally a big leap as an Australian kid? How did you navigate that?

Yeah. It was pretty wild. No one understood a word I said. [*laughs*] I had a really strong accent and Australia was and is like the furthest place from New York. It literally is the other side of the world. So, here I was, this 10, 11, 12-year-old kid sticking out like a sore thumb. But finding my way because as a teenager too, like, it's right when you're looking for independence and, you know, looking to come into yourself.

Did uni come next? Was it Manhattan School of Music or New School?

I was at the New School. At that time, this was 2001, the two big schools in New York were the New School and Manhattan School. Juilliard hadn't set up their jazz program at that stage. And Manhattan School had more of an emphasis on larger ensembles and New School had more of an emphasis on small groups.

And having just played in a big band and larger ensembles for four years, I really gravitated towards the small groups. And there was a lot of spillover between the faculty of Manhattan School and New School. So it was friendly fire, you know, between the two.

And what were you thinking at the time? Were you wanting to become a jazz musician? Were you just pursuing a legitimate jazz education generally? Where was your head at?

At that time, I was pretty dead set on becoming a working saxophone player. I'd been playing and performing for quite some time and my time in high school gave me the confidence to take it seriously. It's what made sense to me and so, I guess my aspirations were just to become a working musician in New York.

Jumping back to high school, I had a very encouraging English teacher who had, unbeknownst to me, put me up for some academic scholarship for a traditional kind of liberal arts East Coast school. She only told me that I had received the scholarship. I hadn't known that my name had been put in the hat.

And I said, "Oh, that's really sweet, but you know, I want to be a musician. I want to study music." And she was so disappointed and upset with me that she called my dad who just like, A, it was quite remarkable that he answered the phone, but, B, he just kind of laughed, you know and was like, "I have nothing to do with where he's gonna go to school or study. That's completely up to him." And it was almost a scandal that I didn't pursue a more traditional college education.

Like doing English as a subject. Is that what she was suggesting?

Which is really funny, because I don't think I can even string a sentence together and I single-handedly keep spellcheck in business, you know.

How long were you at the conservatory for?

I was there for four years. They try with all their power to weed you out after two. They want to trim the fat. And the first two years are quite challenging. You're in something known as the proficiency program. So you have to basically prove your playing, you know, and you get out of proficiency. And after your first two years, you have what's called a sophomore jury, which you have to pass to move forward.

Did you feel pressured by all this? Or was it normal by that point to have to present music to a jury?

It was pressure but it was also friendly fire, and a drive, like everyone knew what they had to do. And we were doing what we wanted to do, and you were there because you wanted to be, you know, so it wasn't necessarily met with resistance.

Were there any teachers there that were especially influential?

Big time. I can't remember if this was my audition or the first day of school jam session, but I remember walking into a room and there stood Reggie Workman on bass — who played with John Coltrane — and that setting the stage, so to speak, of what to expect teacher-wise. Barry Harris, Cecil Bridgewater, Charles Tolliver — all people that I'd only ever seen on the liner notes of records — were now my teachers. To suddenly be in a room with your idols and three other students is pretty extraordinary.

You know, we were really, really lucky and it felt like a continuation of high school in a sense, because the whole concept of higher jazz education is pretty confusing at the best of times, you know? Institutionalizing something which is essentially taught by ear and through practice. It has the potential to go wrong really quickly, but they did a great job of establishing a community and an openness to whatever it is that you were interested in.

Super cool to be able to spend time with idols in a small room setting for hours.

Classes were long, ensemble classes were three hours and we would have class and then you would go across the street with your teacher, have a few drinks and then go back and have another class, which is playing, you know. So we were just playing all day.

And in parallel, are you starting to collect jazz records and are you into other styles of music?

Since being a kid and the family shop, I'd always had a record collection, and had a relationship to physical music in that sense. In high school hip-hop was happening in such an all-encompassing way that I, of course, was drawn and listened obsessively to hip-hop, which I could draw the connection to, to jazz. My time at the New School, it was mostly playing and recording. I was buying records here and there, but it was less, it was also the time. The early 2000s, it happened to be the time of the MP3. So you would go to your friend's house and bring your hard drive and, you know, swap entire discographies.

The wild west of downloading.

The wild west of downloading and ripping, and going to the library at school or at Lincoln Center and ripping and taping. We'd tape everything back then, you know.

"The whole concept of higher jazz education is pretty confusing at the best of times"

I want to talk about your first steps as a DJ. What came first, DJ'ing or working with Mark Ronson?

First DJ steps, I think were, I liked being in control of the music at parties. [*laughs*] I was a bit shy as a kid. And I liked being able to hide behind the music. Towards the end of my four years at the New School, I began to get more and more interested in recording and engineering, and production. And it was through recording and production that I wound up with Mark.

How did meeting Mark come about?

A close friend from high school who was a singer invited me to a gig that she had. And I went. And I noticed there was only maybe six people there. It was, you know, typical New York gig. And one of the people there was Mark who was heckling the drummer. And I had just, at that time, started to see his name on records. So it was a little bit after the Nikka Costa record, and there was a few other bits and pieces floating around. And, I went up to him, and introduced myself and said, you know, "I've just graduated from the New School. If you ever need any help in the studio, give me a call," type of thing. And that was on like a Friday. And then on Monday, I got a voicemail. And I remember it was quite exciting because, this was still, like, the early days of cellphones. And I got a voicemail from Mark saying, "Why don't you come past the studio?" It was round the corner, it was on Mercer Street. And I went. And he just kinda showed me what he was doing, and this was leading up to "Version."

I was gonna ask.

He was working very closely with the Dap-Kings at the time, who I knew through New School. Dave Guy, we went to the same high school, and he went to New School too. [Ronson] showed me what he was doing, and I was so drawn to spending time in the studio. And he said, "Do you just want to come in?" And so I just started going in, and that turned into an assistant role, kind of studio assistant. And kind of jack of all trades. A bit of everything.

Was it through that sample culture, how you found your way discovering music back then?

Absolutely. Again, this is before whosampled.com, you know. You would go to a record store, and I remember I have embarrassingly poor pitch, but like singing my interpretation of songs to find out what they were, you know. Asking people what they were to find out what they are. Or in a sample, maybe you heard a snippet of a vocal, and then you would remember that. Or you would try and track down what that vocal was, or an instrumentation. I would surprise myself with what these samples were, because they were people that I knew, you know, and records that I had actually already known.

Just people interpreting them differently.

Yeah. We were learning the new songs, but I was rediscovering these old songs, which I previously had a different relationship to.

How important was the record store as a site of discovery back then?

It was everything. Going to the record store was a weekly occurrence, and it was where all our pocket money went, you know, at record shops. You wanted to buy records, so you could then play them, and it's like a cycle.

The MP3 was already a thing, but was music on the internet not so catalogued as it is now?

Oh, yeah. Music wasn't as catalogued in a sense, but also, I guess I'm jumping around a bit, but mid-2000s, you had the introduction of the CDJ as a standard piece of equipment in a club, or Serato became a standard. But prior to that, you know, most bars and clubs in New York only had turntables, if that. Like, we would bring turntables to places for a $50 gig, you would lug thousands of dollars worth of equipment, just for this opportunity to play these records that you were excited about.

Did you have a regular gig back then, or were you just finding spots here and there?

It was a lot of here and there. The first regular DJ gig I had was in 2006, with some friends who were all through the studio, through Allido, and we called it Prince Night, and we only played the music of Prince, and Prince affiliates.

So you had partners in crime?

I think actually through playing music, and through being in bands, I really found an importance in being with other people, and it not being a solo experience. So I enjoyed playing records with other people. It made it more interactive, more of a conversation, more interesting.

How long did you assist him for?

I was at Allido for maybe a year. And that was 2006. And whilst there, the in-house engineer was a guy named Derek Pacuk, who, generously, really showed me the ropes. You know, like, before sessions, after sessions, would show me little things in Pro Tools. Told me how to set the studio up. And I ate all of that up. I really ate it up. And alongside the production was DJ'ing, you know.

And Mark had been DJ'ing a lot in those days. And I was going out more, and, it was through that, that I kind of fell into DJ'ing more, you know. At its essence though it was still just wanting to control the music at a party. That's all it ever is, really.

Were you playing hip-hop at the beginning? How would you describe what you were playing?

In the beginning, it was hip-hop and breaks. And those were the records that I had. I was learning that the majority of the jazz records, and I started buying more soul records at that time, had samples on them.

And I obsessively would look for the sample of new hip-hop that came out, and of hip-hop that I liked. It was really just about discovering the sample. And finding breaks. So, my first venture into that world was playing music that I was comfortable with, you know, that I knew.

"At its essence though it was still just wanting to control the music at a party. That's all it ever is, really."

Is this around the time where East Village Radio started happening, where you started doing a show?

Yeah. So, Mark had a show, and I remember the first time he asked me to sub for him, I was terrified, but immediately drawn to the performative aspect of radio, especially live radio. And doubly so, because East Village Radio was located on the street. It was this glass booth on 1st [Street] and 1st [Avenue]. And so purely by nature of the fact that there's only a piece of glass between you and the sidewalks of New York City, it was a little bit more performative. So I subbed for Mark a couple of times, I then spent some time at Wax Poetics, and helped them setting up their reissue label. They were invited by East Village Radio to do a show. And I was the co-host, with my friend Rios. And that was 2007, it was the Wax Poetics Record Rundown.

And then East Village Radio invited us to have our own show, which wound up being after Mark's, in some incredible karmic, cosmic turn of events. So we were Friday nights, and that was 2008 that "Never Not Working" was born. The joke was that in 2008 when we started it, we didn't have traditional jobs. We were playing, we were recording, we were doing stuff, and we like to refer to it as work even though it wasn't in the traditional sense. So it was this very tongue-in-cheek, poke, "We're working," you know, and here's a double negative to prove it.

Was this every week that you did a show?

It was every week. I look back and it's like, I'm exhausted just thinking about it. But every week we did a show and we either had a guest or a theme and then most likely, after we played the show, we would go and play a party. It was like the jumping-off point. So Friday night was like, OK, do the show, and then maybe we would somehow schlep over to Brooklyn or run around the corner and play a quick set. Or if we had a guest, they might want to do that, it kept going, it started on a Friday night and it would keep going.

That must've taken a lot of preparation and music discovery. Was finding new stuff to play a priority back then?

Absolutely. It kept me going, it kept me record shopping, wanting to find records for the show. There was a difference between playing records on the show and then playing records out at parties and clubs, because it started as more of a traditional mix show and kind of upbeat, but it is a different medium and it led me into buying records for different reasons, which was a huge learning curve for me; buying a record to play on the show versus buying a record for any other number of reasons.

And then East Village Radio closed down and you moved on to doing a show at Red Bull. Can you talk about what the idea was behind the Red Bull show?

Yeah. So when EVR shut down for the first time in 2014, it felt like this void that could never be filled, you know, it was really like, "What are we going to do?" Like, what's going to happen? And it happened to be this funny timing, right? When Red Bull had set up their permanent studio, and it gave birth to Red Bull Studios, Red Bull Radio, Red Bull Arts, and Joe, who had been at East Village Radio, invited me over to Red Bull. And said, you know, "Would you be interested in having a show here." And I thought, well, it shouldn't be the same show. It should be a different show. And I was going to be doing it by myself. So I thought to change it, I didn't feel like I needed to play records. And I liked other people playing records as the catalyst for conversation, and either talking about how those records came to that person, their involvement with them, their relationship with them, you know, and it wasn't limited to just DJs and musicians or producers. It was all sorts of creative people, and they're talking about their relationship to music.

So it was an opportunity to open things up to a wider array of guests.

Yeah. It was an opportunity to open things up, to explore a different aspect to it, to kind of venture into a new headspace a little bit. And whilst EVR, like the show there, the emphasis had been on playing music, this felt like an opportunity for the emphasis to be on talking about music.

And then Red Bull crossed over with the Lot Radio starting.

Yes. That was around the same time. And the Lot invited me over there. And I wasn't sure. I thought, well, it should be different again, you know. Maybe it should be a different approach. So then it kind of reshifted back onto more of an emphasis on music, rather than talk. And I think that has to do with the fact that it's outside. You're seeing people, it's more performative. Not to mention, you're on camera.

"A record kind of represents music in its entirety in itself, because the record doesn't exist alone, it exists as a part of such a bigger thing."

Whereas Red Bull was in a room upstairs.

In a room, in a studio. There's an engineer in the corner. It's a completely different vibe.

Did you see those shows as an opportunity, or almost a responsibility to create a platform for your friends and wider artistic network to come on, and be featured?

Certainly with East Village Radio, you know, there was a real sense of community, not only with our show, but with all shows, you know, there was friends of the show and kind of this "through association" type of thing. And a lot of guests came to us through friends. So and so knew that this person was going to be in town this weekend so why don't they stop on the show.

Anyone from, you know, Bob James, to Rhymefest, heroes of ours who we wanted to introduce to a wider audience. At Red Bull, the show itself, the fact that it was more of a discussion, that dictated the type of people. And it opened it up to a wider audience both in listenership and guest selection. I think a big part of it was, I was growing with these shows, so my taste grew and changed and my involvement in music changed, and my relationship to it changed.

Has your music discovery changed over the years from record store-based discovering and listening to the radio to online?

Yeah, I mean, I listen to shows online now. And I think a common thread though being, and this is my good friend Andy's, this is his quote. It's, "The sound that you like, but songs you don't know yet." And that kind of rings true. There's a sound that I know that I gravitate towards, and resonates with me, and I kind of search for that sound as a form of discovery. And there's no shortage. There's an infinite amount of music that already exists. It's a never-ending pursuit, if you want it to be.

Do you care about formats? Do you care about getting your music as a vinyl record, a cassette, a digital file?

I used to, I used to be very, very particular about format. With age and with space and with, you know, back problems and stairs and travel and convenience and all sorts of things, I'm less particular now.

And you can have the same kind of deep listening environment with a digital file as with a record that you put on?

Yes, for me, totally. The listening happens within the ears, you know, it doesn't happen outside. And

I really respect the audiophile approach. I respect that other people have different relationships to it. To me, it happens within, it doesn't happen outwardly.

Has the importance of physical vinyl records lessened for you over the years?

Well, I'll contradict myself here and say no, because a record, the physicality of the record, one, produces a sound, which isn't reproducible. But two, having the cover art, and the information about the recording, having that at your fingertips is something that I missed. And I think that's very important. At least for me, I'm interested in who is playing, where they played, who was involved, you know, I find it fascinating, the album artwork choices, if it's related to the music, if it's completely not related to the music, it's equally interesting. And, "Oh, they chose to print it like this." I do find that interesting.

The vinyl records you hang on to now, are they more sentimental in your connection to them?

Yes. I have the same relationship to books as I do with records, I find it very hard to get rid of [them]. I might not be interested in it at this particular moment, but that's not to say that I might not then think of it at another time. I find revisiting the collection really fun and useful.

More often than not, there's a story of how any record came to me, and that one, whether it's a story of how that record came to me, or this record is on this same label as this, you know, or this producer, or these musicians, it's not just one record. A record kind of represents music in its entirety in itself, because the record doesn't exist alone, it exists as a part of such a bigger thing. Keeping them, or having a relationship to it is in a way, having a relationship to something which is much larger than the record itself. It's having a relationship to the music, the story.

Let's chat about I Should Care Records. This was your first record label?

It was, yes.

How did it come about and what was the ethos about it?

After, or alongside being involved in radio, and alongside hosting a radio show, and being part of a community of musicians, record labels were synonymous within that community. And just part of the culture that existed, I Should Care is pretty tongue-in-cheek in that it was, well, I'd spent a lot of energy focused on sharing and learning about older music.

I should care about new music and contemporary music, and I should care about sharing it, and I should care about what's going on. Short-lived, yet it kind of naturally evolved into Book Works.

Did you learn a lot from doing I Should Care, going through the motions of producing a record and then producing cassettes and stuff? Was that your first experience actually doing the production of all that?

I'd worked on the engineering, recording side before, but from a label perspective, actually making a record and getting something mastered, I'd never been in charge of that myself. I learnt very quickly that when there's a word that follows music, whether it's music business or the music industry or management or anything like that, I became less interested. It changes the relationship very quickly, you know? And you needed to think about other things. Primarily the moment that money and music are being spoken about at the same time, it can get complicated.

So then after some time, you start Book Works. Do you want to talk about the origin story of Book Works, how that all came about?

It was quite unexpected. Martin [Davis] and I were neighbors and a neighborly nod slash stop and chat on the street, kind of grew into, "Oh, we have friends in common," you know. And we quickly discovered we both had an affinity towards jazz, like first and foremost. Martin is very knowledgeable in the world of jazz, both musically and visually, and we really enjoy talking about it. And we would just talk and that led to having ideas of, "Oh, well, this could be interesting, or what if we did this," and it really just started as three T-shirts, the Deodato, the Sonny Rollins, and the Wes Montgomery tee. And we weren't expecting the response that we received. So, "Oh if other people are going to take this seriously, we should take this seriously too." And that was the origin of Book Works.

> "Take the R out of brand and you have band, and I feel more comfortable thinking of it as a band and that there are band members, and my role can vary."

So you were surprised by the reaction? Was Book Works a hobby project in its inception? Was the intention from the beginning for it to be a side thing?

It's parallel with I Should Care. So on one hand I was interested in recording and putting out music. Martin was exploring and discovering a visual identity. And the two things lined up cosmically. We were humbled by the response and how it was received. It was our friends at first who encouraged us and who responded to it. We kind of didn't want to limit it to just clothing. T-shirts were a great way to get an idea across, communicate something, but there was, and there still is an interest across multimedia, whether it be records or T-shirts or objects, that can act as a vehicle for an idea and kind of tap into something.

And was producing T-shirts, sweatshirts, and hoodies, stuff like that the most practical way of going about starting something, more than records, perhaps?

To do a run of vinyl, you've got to meet a minimum pressing requirement. And then breaking even is a success. And T-shirts, it felt less personal. With records and tapes, if there was not a response, it didn't have to be a positive response, but I take it very personally. And there was something in the shift of medium, which was a little less serious, a little more playful.

I'm still surprised to be doing what I'm doing and feel incredibly lucky to do so. I don't necessarily think of it as a brand. Take the R out of brand and you have band, and I feel more comfortable thinking of it as a band and that there are band members, and my role can vary. But whatever happens, the T-shirt, the hoodie, the record, whatever it might be, is a chance to convey an idea.

You take a really specific jazz reference that might have quite a niche audience, and you put it on a T-shirt, which is a widely appealing medium.

There's something very democratic about it, and I draw a parallel to radio, in that there's an educational aspect, and you're sharing perhaps a piece of very specific knowledge through a T-shirt. Which then can lead people to ask questions, or reach their own conclusions, or have their own ideas. And that's the best possible scenario, to me, that's the same as hopefully doing an interesting radio show, is that you challenge the listener to think about something. A favorite of mine, my high school bandleader Bob Stewart used to refer to Art Blakey and the Jazz Messengers as university on the corner of Lennox Avenue. He used to say that. And so, I heard that as a kid, and it just stayed in my head. And then one day, Martin and I were looking for parking, which is always an adventure in New York, and it just kind of popped back into my head. I said, "Oh, what about UCLA? University on the corner of Lennox Avenue?" And then it was like, "OK, that's an idea, let's just list the members." Again, the tongue-in-cheek thing, liberating the UCLA from its college affiliation. And that's how a lot of the ideas come about, it's kind of an inside joke, or knowledge learned through recording, or through understanding the history.

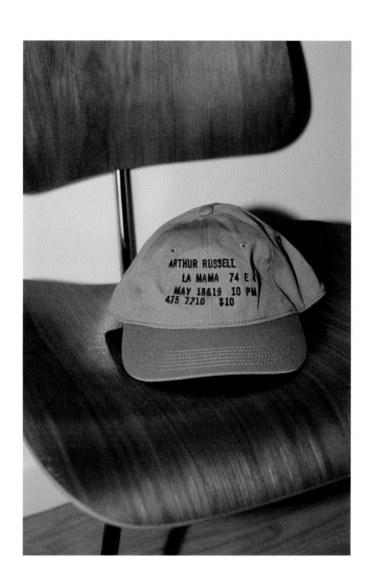

"I find practice to be a really beautiful concept, in and of itself. Whatever it is that you're practicing, practice is important."

Putting an unlikely and specific reference on clothing is appealing in itself?

I think so. Hopefully it's appealing. For Book Works I think it's fun, it's really about this idea of bebop specifically, but hard-bop, post-bop, straight-ahead, contemporary jazz, is all built upon the American Songbook. Like the jazz repertoire is built on chord changes to songs which existed already. Musicians in the '40s, '50s, and '60s found that the chord changes were what was interesting. It wasn't necessarily these melodies, it's the chord changes which give them the opportunity to play, and to explore through solos. So, what the jazz repertoire is, Book Works hopes to do the same thing. It's like we're taking the chord changes, but then we're putting a melody on top, or we're rewriting a melody, or we're reharmonizing these chord changes that already exist, so reharmonizing an idea visually.

What does the Works part of Book Works signify?

Yeah, the American Songbook, and fake books. Fake books were these widely circulated books which started in the '70s for conservatory students. It's this given that you need to learn these songs if you're playing gigs with musicians that you don't know. If a song is called, you need to be able to play it, and so you'd learn these songs. This is the language, this is the lexicon, it's the repertoire, it's something you have to know.

Work, in the sense that you need to practice. And accomplishing something only comes through practice and it's not a god-given right that you're going to know these chord changes or these melodies, it's through practice. And I find practice to be a really beautiful concept, in and of itself. Whatever it is that you're practicing, practice is important. So, Book Works being again this tongue-in-cheek, nod to these ideas of putting in work, reexamining something that already exists. We're not reinventing the wheel by any means, but we're just thinking about it from a different angle.

What is the process of coming up with ideas for graphics? Are there enough inside jokes to make a whole collection every couple of months?

The inside joke might be that it is only inside jokes. [*laughs*] Levels of inside jokes. I have started to think

about it more seasonally now, like what would suit itself maybe to a sweatshirt or a hoodie or a jacket rather than a T-shirt. But, the idea is, maybe there's one idea which then in thinking about that leads to others. There's certainly no formula and there's no set procedure on how they come about. It's really just one idea and then what would be a nice pairing. In that sense, it's really the same as pulling records for a radio show or for a set. Once you start with that first record or the first song selection, that almost dictates everything that comes after. And the first thing doesn't exist without the things that come after. So it's a bit of that approach really.

There's also personal graphics that come from your own personal history, like your granddad's record shop.

Yep, exactly. So the angel playing the lute was painted on the side of the window of the house I grew up in. So it was this image that I saw for most of my life. And I had a very sentimental relationship to. And then one day, I found an old newspaper ad for Discurio, and thought, "Why not?" There's been a few of those and a few graphics or a few ideas, which are love letters to the past, whether it be a personal connection or through folklore or through osmosis or anything.

You talked about the brand being a band. Who to date has the band consisted of and who were some of the regular collaborators?

There are several people who kind of come in and out. Toya [Horiuchi], Alix [Gutiérrez], Elijah [Anderson], are all regular band members. And even if they're not playing on the record, they're present. It's very important that it's band driven, it's democratic and band-driven decisions. Sometimes people will bring something to the table, which I view as like suggesting a song. Like, "Maybe we wanna try this song. Maybe we want to record this. Could this be interesting?" And then we think about it that way. Other times it's ideas that I have or that other band members help execute. Like maybe this person is better at this specific thing, so why not, let that person shine.

"I can say when I was practicing regularly, I had the best sleep of my life. There weren't the burning questions or anxieties within. Practicing and playing answered questions I didn't know I had."

And that analogy to the bandleader, you took on literally when you did the "Book Works Trio EP"?

Yeah. That was a fun exercise of like, wanting to do a record, but wanting it to purely be about the music and nothing else. And, in that sense, I was a bit of a bandleader who subbed in for percussion.

Is that the ultimate project for you within Book Works, to record and release music, or just one part?

It's one part, and it's a part that I think is important and that I'm working on at the moment, alongside the visual component. It's important to exercise your ears. The musical aspect is of equal importance.

You've been a sponge to music and culture from a really young age. Do you feel with Book Works, you've finally found a way to convert that specific interest in different musical styles and whatnot into something that appeals to a wider audience? Have you found a way to work with the lexicon in your mind?

I'm hesitant to say, "Oh, I've found it."

Yeah, I might be being too revelatory...

Like "this is it." But Book Works feels like the amalgamation of a lot of information that I've retained, or, as you say, like, as a sponge, absorbed. And I'm encouraged that with its reception, you know, I find it encouraging. I'm still practicing, you know. It's still a form of practice.

And have you picked up a saxophone in a while?

The last time I picked it up was to play "Happy Birthday" for my wife. [*laughs*] I have a standing request in September to play "Happy Birthday." But embarrassingly, I haven't picked it up in a while. I think about it all the time. But I find it easier to sit down at a piano than I do to pick up the saxophone at the moment.

Is the playing of an instrument still integral to your life?

I don't wanna fake the funk. So I think it's important and I can say when I was practicing regularly, I had the best sleep of my life. There weren't the burning questions or anxieties within. Practicing and playing answered questions I didn't know I had. It is important to me.

A lot of people get into DJ'ing or production without formal music training or understanding of music in its detail, like chord structures and notation and stuff. Does that give you a different perspective on all of this?

I think it gives my ear a different perspective, for sure. You know, I hear things differently, and then, because I hear things differently, I gravitate towards different things for different reasons. It's a two-sided coin though because having studied and understanding the theory and the technical limitations of music, and of recording, it's very hard to not be analytical. It's hard for me not to be in ear training class, and to transcribe and analyze, because that's what I studied to do, to analyze music. I try very hard to now analyze and have a relationship to feeling. And that's where that whole notion of, "You know you like it." The sounds that you like, but the songs you don't know yet. And again, it's that you can't quite put a finger on what the feeling is that is evoked with music, but you know it's important, and you know it's stronger than yourself, and therefore to me, should be taken seriously. That's not to say it can't be fun or playful or anything else, but it also should be taken seriously. It's hard for me to detach as a listener, that can be a challenge.

Because you've been on both sides of the fence?

Yeah. I feel like I've danced around it, I'm dancing around the fire and it's — I guess I want to say something about feeling really fortunate though, to have an understanding, to approach it in the way I do. I feel beyond fortunate. It's the one thing that makes sense to me. The world of finance doesn't make sense to me, you know, I can't quite understand it. The world of architecture, I can't quite wrap my head around it. But I do recognize the power of music and the importance that it plays. And it being something that's just larger than one person. **R**

CONDITIONS

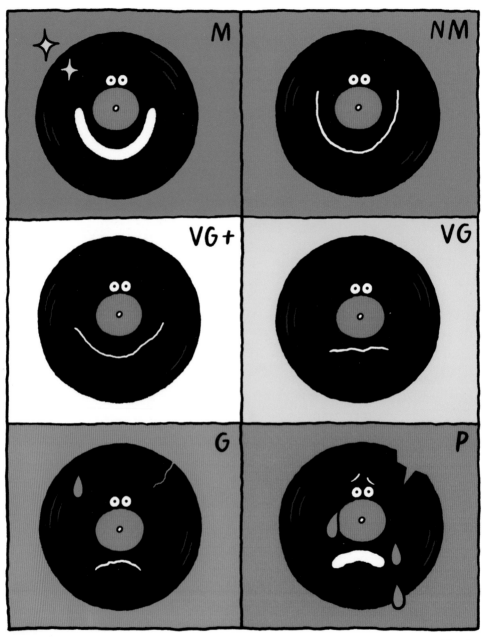

Redlich